A Woman's Guide to Prime Time Dating

Sept 97.

If you have $20,000.000
and nice I am Single.

$15,000 000 TO MY new X
$4000.000 FOR ME
you keep the rest.

if you have over $50.000000
you do not have to be
nice.
If you have over $100.000.000.
you do not even have
to be female.

Victor

A Woman's Guide to Prime Time Dating

For the Woman

Who Wasn't Born Yesterday

by Gloria Bledsoe Goodman

A Lyle Stuart Book

Published by Carol Publishing Group

A Lyle Stuart Book
Published by Carol Publishing Group

Editorial Offices
600 Madison Avenue
New York, NY 10022

Sales & Distribution Offices
120 Enterprise Avenue
Secaucus, NJ 07094

In Canada: Musson Book Company
A division of General Publishing Co. Ltd.

Manufactured in the United States of America

10 9 8 7 6 5 4 3 2 1

Carol Publishing Group books are available at special discounts
for bulk purchases, for sales promotions, fund raising, or
educational purposes. Special editions can also be created to
specifications. For details contact: Special Sales Department,
Carol Publishing Group, 120 Enterprise Ave., Secaucus, NJ 07094

Library of Congress Cataloging-in-Publication Data

Goodman, Gloria Bledsoe.
    A woman's guide to prime time dating / by Gloria Bledsoe Goodman.
        p. cm.
    "A Lyle Stuart book."
    ISBN 0-8184-0531-7
    1. Dating (Social customs) 2. Middle aged women—United States.
I. Title.
HQ801.G592   1990
646.7'7—dc20
                                                           90-43762
                                                             CIP

To my beloved Inner Core trio; to the nine A-Team Tasters who are fearless tasters of life as well as of food, and all the ladies who cared enough to share the pleasures and the pains of mid-life mating with me. You know who you are. And my everlasting thanks to my daughter, Linda Ross Becker, without whose assistance this book would have never happened.

I am very grateful to the many people who have given generously of their time to help me with this project. A special thanks to Norma and Mike Slover, personal growth counselors in Salem, Oregon; Rev. Willis Steinberg, former vicar and family counselor at St. Paul's Episcopal Church, Salem; Rev. Steve Bearden, assistant pastor and marriage and family therapist at First Church of the Nazarene in Salem; B. J. Seymour, social worker, Portland, Oregon; Kay Mitchell, my eagle-eyed copy editor in Salem; and Allan Wilson, my editor at Carol Publishing Group. A special thanks to my agent, Pema Browne of Pema Browne Ltd, New York City, whose enthusiastic support and friendship helped me every step of the way.

CONTENTS

INTRODUCTION

The divorce decree is signed. You no longer look over that numbing document wondering tearfully when the love, honor, and cherish began to fade. You've long since stopped hoping that close scrutiny of that document would erase the two names once joined so lovingly on another document—a marriage license. You just don't care much anymore.

The refrain of "What did she do that I didn't do?" no longer rises to haunt you when you awake at 4 A.M. Remarkably, you no longer awake at 4 A.M. You arise at a reasonable hour and feel relatively calm and rested for the day ahead.

Perhaps you are a woman in different circumstances. The death certificate is filed and tucked away in the family Bible. For you, the funeral marked the end of a relationship that spanned some of your girlhood and much of your womanhood.

Friends call, but not quite so often. When they do call, it's to make dates for daytime lunches. They do not include you in their dinner plans.

And maybe some of you suffered through the terrible day when the secretary of your couples bridge club called to ask if you had any replacements in mind for your seats. Well, of course, bridge is played in multiples of two. You knew that, so why does it hurt so much? Couldn't they have asked you to bring a woman friend?

Sorry, dear. It just doesn't work that way. Women friends turn strange when one in their midst is suddenly single. Automatically, a widow becomes competition even though you wouldn't have their Edwin on a silver salver. Your women friends begin to worry that Edwin might like you on a silver salver, so they see you only at safe women-only events.

After the flush of these first painful rejections fade, you turn sensible and set resolutions. There's a powerful determination to go it alone. I've had my life *à deux*, you think. It's over. A woman my age doesn't have to have male companionship, you reason. I'll devote my life to my grandchildren; do good works, go out with woman friends and learn to make ragout out of the chopped liver my life has become.

But, despite these brave resolves, a day comes when you notice there is something definitely missing in your life. There are changes within you. Changes made evident by perhaps a tiny tug at your womanly vitals, a little quiver, a blush to the cheeks and a mad desire to giggle at the postman's oft-told jokes. What is this? You are an adult, a grown-up woman, a grandmother.

The fact, my dear, whether you realize it or not, is that you are in the process of reentry. You are about to rejoin the race of normal functioning women. You're beginning to think of men as men again and not as departed but precious memories or as cheating potbellied rats on bird legs. Admit it, you'd really relish a bit of the remarkable mystique, the challenge which builds between the male and female as they go through the ritual dance of dating, courtship and companionship.

Whether the loss of your mate was due to death or dishonor or maybe even your own choice, you are a woman, and like most of us, you eventually began to realize that life without a man is like having the whole enchilada without salsa.

So what if you're 40-ish, 50-ish, or 60-ish-plus? You're ready to enter the mainstream once more. You are ready to go out with men even though you haven't had a date since 1948, and that one resulted in marriage, three children, and lots of living, both good and bad.

How can you as a mid-life grandmother send out signals that you are ready, available and a whole lot smarter than you were in 1948?

Steady on. Don't plunge. You've got to survey the terrain.

The first horrible truth you're going to discover is that in today's society, it's a buyer's market and, alas, the buyers are all male.

That's the bad news. The good news is that with proper marketing and an entirely new attitude on life, love, and the world around you, you can reenter the ark—as in two by two together.

The good memories of your marriage will never fade as long as you live, but that's exactly what you must begin to do—live.

This book is a step-by-step mid-life mating manual to get you back into the mainstream of life. And don't skip a chapter. You might miss something.

CHAPTER 1

THE BONUS YEARS

What Are You Going to Do with the Rest of Your Life?

You've spent the first part of your life being a kid. The second, and by far the longest period of your existence on this planet, has been dedicated to your husband and your children. Suddenly the rules are changed, and you find yourself facing the third part—the rest of your life. And Part III belongs to you—the mid-life woman—to do exactly with as you want.

So what are going to do with the bonus years our grandmothers rarely had time to enjoy? You can take up the painting that couldn't be squeezed in when you were ferrying kids to and from Little League and ballet lessons. You can take a class in conversational French which you may never use but sounds like fun. You can, well, you can be yourself. It's your turn.

When your period of grieving is over, and your marriage is but a memory, you may decide you want a man in your life again. Life is out there waiting to be lived, but remember that old adage: Be careful what you wish for because you may get it.

You have some decisions to make. Pay attention. This is serious stuff. We're talking about the rest of your life.

Every human being has needs. Even the most primitive of tribes have vital but basic requirements. Food, shelter and clothing are their needs, but even primitives are driven to take the hum-drum out of routine activities. They embellish everyday chores with elaborate and time-honored rituals. They dance before a hunt, and they chant when the hunters return triumphant. The women sing as they go about their jobs, often centuries-old chants that are related to the tasks at hand. The reaching of adulthood by adolescents often calls for a dramatic act of proof followed by a village celebration.

But other than these basic decisions—go hunting? stay in? plant grain now? wait until next week?—the primitives rarely make decisions about their own destiny. Their roles are pre-defined by centuries of tradition. Life for these people is a road map with all the stops checked, death being the ultimate expected destination for all.

There are no records of primitives losing sleep over whether or not they are fulfilled in their lives or whether their partners answer their emotional and physical needs. Ambition, if there is any, takes simple forms.

We, of course, are not primitive unless thrown into dire circumstances. Most of us are lucky enough to be able to take for granted the basics of food, shelter, and clothing. And sex for us is—fortunately—more often recreation rather than procreation. Our life-styles leave us the leisure to think. Ordinarily this is a great blessing, but occasionally it becomes a curse. When a person is given time to think, there is a tendency to think, often to excess, about one's self.

Except for you, of course. Because you're a caring female, you haven't taken the time to think about yourself for years. You've been too busy being a wife and mother. Unless we are spoiled rotten, most women go from girlhood to womanhood to motherhood thinking of others. At the beginning of the experience called marriage, the life stretching before us seems an endless ribbon of time, and we think it will forever stay the same. We are wives, we are lovers, we are mothers, we are daughters, we are caretakers, and in the last two decades, many of us have added the title of breadwinner or co-breadwinner to our resume.

We, the mid-life women, have had little or no time for self-nurturing because our own needs have constantly been displaced by the needs of others. This has been our life, the way of the world as our mothers and grandmothers before us have known it. Although we occasionally may have railed against the inequity, we have worked within this system because it is a woman's nature to be a caretaker.

The "Me" and "I" angst of today's younger women are alien thought processes to contemporary grandmothers because assessments of our own needs were already formed before the feminist movement took firm root. We'll talk more about the mid-life woman and the feminist movement in a later chapter. We're talking decisions here.

A young co-worker once asked me, "When you get sick, do you want your mother?" I could have laughed, but she was so serious, I only could answer, "I am the mother." This was not a self-pitying remark; it was simply the truth as I lived it for most of my life.

Personally, I have always been convinced that womankind is at least twenty thousand years more evolved than mankind because of our incredible ability to shift ourselves into whatever is needed at that particular time—often assuming more than one identity simultaneously to satisfy the needs of our husband, our children, our parents, our employers and our community.

Then, just as suddenly as it all began, the life you have lived since marriage is over. There may come a day when you find yourself, by reasons of divorce or death, left alone.

You have been abandoned. You feel wretched. You are angry. You are devastated. Take heart. You are a woman, and therefore, you will deal with the loss more rationally, says the Rev. Steve Bearden of the First Nazarene Church of Salem, Oregon.

Bearden, who holds degrees in theology and marriage and family therapy, conducts workshops on easing the pain of divorce. After dealing with hundreds of divorced people, Bearden has discovered that women are more willing to feel pain and learn to deal with it than men are. When women do heal after a mate is lost, they heal more completely.

"Man's answer to the loss is to jump right into

another relationship. It's a quick fix," he said. "In extreme cases, men will hop into one relationship after another because new relationships offer challenges and stop the pain. But this is not reality. Women are more ready to say, 'I hurt. What can I do about it?' "

So, although life may have thrown you a twister, there is no reason to believe that your own particular soap opera has been cancelled.

Children will be loving and caring after the death or defection of their father. If they are mature adults, they even will try to understand if you were the one who chose the divorce. But because you realize that no person should ever be completely responsible for another person's happiness, you will, in time, lovingly distance yourself from their devoted scrutiny and begin to make your own decisions about your future. It is, after all, your future.

Making a decision sounds deceptively simple, but is isn't if you are, as the French say "of that certain age." Unlike younger women, most of us over fifty—unless we have always been extremely strong and assertive—have had most of the major decisions in our lives made by a man.

We couldn't help it. Correction: We could help it, but we chose not to. We were taught by example that we needed a man to validate our existence. By the time we ceased being Daddy's girl, we were Hubby's wife—unless we became spinsters, a dreaded state in those days.

In our marriages, our roles were so clearly defined that we rarely dared to deviate. We were the keepers of the home flame, the distaff side of the marriage, this

designation made centuries before we were born because women's hands plied the distaff, which held the
flax or wool during spinning.

If we were fortunate in our choice of men, we had a
rational husband with whom to make decisions. If we
were not so fortunate, we made do with what we had
chosen. It was our bed to lie upon.

To many women our age, divorce was a stigma—
something other people did. The legal action to dissolve
a marriage was a public acknowledgement of a personal
failure; therefore, it was, for many of us, out of the
question.

Even those who had rational husbands with whom
to discuss problems rarely had the final vote. Like the
good little girls we'd been taught to be, we put our own
desires behind those of our husbands and our children.

Take Betty Jean. The word "I" was missing from
her vocabulary, unless it was prefaced by "should" or
followed by "will be glad to."

Betty Jean's father had been killed in an oil rig fire
in Texas. Her mother remarried during World War II,
leaving the teenager with grandparents. At 18, Betty
Jean chose marriage over college because she fell in love
with a pair of deep blue eyes, black curly hair and the
confident manner of an ex-Marine who had seen the
world. She had her first baby at 19, another at 20, and
another at 21. Her world was made up with worries
about why she couldn't breast feed her children, how to
keep her home and children clean enough for a mother-
in-law who made white glove inspections whenever
possible, and how to make $15 stretch for seven days of
food. You could do it in 1952, but it wasn't easy.

By the time Betty Jean was 37 years old, she had

moved twenty-one times because Peripatetic Paul, the handsome ex-Marine, was a hard worker with itchy feet. He changed jobs every eighteen months as he followed electronic contracts throughout Southern California during the fifties.

Betty Jean had her third child while her husband was on the graveyard shift at Northrop Aviation in a Los Angeles suburb. The couple just had arrived from the Deep South, their 1946 Ford straining to pull a thirty-five foot trailer house. The idea of a home on wheels appealed to Paul, who thought the mobility would be just the ticket. Betty Jean was eight months pregnant and had only contacted her doctor once, so she was totally unprepared for the labor pains which came while Paul was at work. She ironed his shirts for the rest of the week, packed her nightcase and called the wife of the trailer court manager. This kindly woman called Paul and arranged for the other two children to be cared for by a woman Betty Jean had met only once.

Eight months after this birth, Paul made a unilateral job move that took them to a dilapidated farmhouse near Edwards Air Force Base in the California desert. The trailer house had been sold, but there was little money left after the move. After the smog of Los Angeles, Betty Jean loved the fresh air of the desert and the yard for her babies to play in, but the farmhouse was a desolate spot.

"One of the down points in my life was the first night in that farmhouse," Betty Jean said. "Paul had gone off to work, it was his first night on the job. We'd arrived late, and there wasn't time for me to go to the store. We were miles from nowhere. All I could find to eat was one can of pumpkin pie filling. I remember trying to convince my three little kids that it was a nice pumpkin pudding. The babies and I sat on pillows around a packing box covered with a dish towel.

"I felt like I was living a *Grapes of Wrath* scenario, and it was one of my life's loneliest moments," said Betty Jean. At least she thought that was the low point of her life—until her husband took off with a secretary half Betty Jean's 52 years. After thirty-four years of marriage, Paul decided marriage was stifling his creativity, and he "needed room to breathe."

This normally buoyant, "can face anything" brunette spent several years racked with excruciating guilt about what what was it that she should have done, but didn't do. Betty Jean has done a lot of growing up in the past two years, and she has learned a lot about herself and life through introspection and counseling.

After two years, the pain has lessened. She has been busy with a garden she planted herself and has been able to watch grow. She is shopping in stores where people know and use her name. She can plan six months ahead.

Of course, she misses Paul. Like the little girl with the curl in the middle of her forehead, Paul was very good when he was good, but when he was bad he was horrid. Betty Jean has learned to live with the understanding that Paul was one type of person, and she was most definitely another.

If you are a believer in star signs, aggressive go-get-'em Paul was a typical Aries needing constant stimulation and challenge, while home-loving Betty Jean was a Virgo who enjoyed a more orderly existence. An astrologer once told her that Aries men and Virgo women should never even shake hands, much less be involved in a marriage for thirty-four years.

I asked her what she wanted for the rest of her life.

"I want to spend Christmas in the same place for five years running," she said.

"With what kind of man?" I asked.

"With a man who knows how to put a Christmas tree in a stand."

Lest I make Betty Jean sound like a simpleton, she most definitely is not. She is simplifying her desires because she knows very well what she wants, and she's tired of complications.

Betty Jean wants marriage with a man who will stay in one place except for an occasional Sunday drive, and will always be around when she wakes up in the morning. She's been a giver up until now, and although she still wants to give, she's ready to receive. Simple give and take is something many women take for granted, but not Betty Jean.

For thirty-four years she squirmed under Paul's dominant thumb, and now she wants a man to be equal partners with her. She wants to sit down and rationally discuss vacation plans. Because she adores her grandchildren, she'd appreciate a man who adores his, so together they can form a new family unit.

For the Betty Jeans of our world, the way is clear. Do you known what you really want?

Do you really need a good old Billy Bob when you think you want a Rod the Rambler, complete with Gucci bag packed-for-travel?

Have you discovered who you are? Not you the wife, nor you the mother. You the woman. If you have, and are ready to proceed with your life, here are some tips offered by Mike and Norma Slover, private practice counselors in Salem, Oregon.

First, make a list outlining the qualities and characteristics most important to you. What does this list tell you? Do you value steadiness and strength above playfulness and gregariousness? Is an outdoorsman more attractive to you than a bookish one? Are you looking for a good companion or a good lover? With luck, you'll get the latter two in one cuddly package because a good companion/friend is just as important as a tender lover to women of the middle years. As couples grow older they are together more, so it is essential that they blend well together, Norma Slover said.

Here are more soul-searching questions to ask yourself before you seek a relationship:

(1) Do you want to be independent? If you do, then seek out a man who will allow you this freedom. Many older men don't understand independence. They are used to being the provider, and they may resent a woman taking her own stand.

(2) Have you given yourself time to grieve properly? The Slovers advise not to rush into any important legal or emotional contract within one year, at least, preferably two, after losing a loved one by either divorce or death.

(3) How accepting are you of the aging process? Should you be called upon, are you ready to take on the role of nurse? For some this might be a repeat performance of a tragedy. Could you bear up under another long illness? How is your own health?

(4) Are you a nurturer? Or do you want to be nurtured?

(5) Are you sure you know what you want? Do you think you want marriage, or do you just want a fling? Note: Don't make any firm decisions about this one. What may begin as a fling may turn into something much deeper.

I'll say it again: Be careful what you wish for, because you may get it.

Annie got what she thought she wanted. This quiet caterpillar of a lady secretly chafed to become a butterfly, and she didn't take the time after the funeral to sit down and think seriously about what she needed to keep her happy.

Life with her Harvey had been completely predictable. From the moment she got up in the morning and fixed breakfast—always two eggs over easy, two strips of bacon, fresh orange juice, toast, medium brown toast, and strong coffee with lots of cream—until she Oil of Olayed her face at night, every second of Annie's day followed a well-traveled route.

Evening never varied. Harvey liked a constant transfusion of news into his veins. Nightly, he sat before the set, watching Cable News Network, his eyes glued to the moment's late-breaking tragedy. Annie really liked a bit of everything. Given her own TV set she would have turned it on to "Wheel of Fortune" and "Lives of the Rich and Famous." But, of course, there was only one TV, and Harvey held the remote control.

A psychiatrist might have been able to tell Harvey that his constant preoccupation with the news was his way of coping with mortality. Bad things always happened to other people. But Harvey, of course, would never have been able to attend counseling sessions to improve his marriage. "What's wrong with it anyway?" was his question when Annie timidly suggested a session.

Harvey died of a heart attack with the TV control clicker in his hand. After the funeral, Annie tossed it in the garbage.

Of course, she had loved Harvey. He was her first love, right out of high school. But now he was dead, and she wanted to live.

A perky redhead who was 59 but looked 45 in a dim light, Annie decided she was ready to enter, maybe not the fastest lane, but one removed from the slow coach thoroughfare.

"I joined several volunteer groups in our town, and I met Gerald at a booster club meeting. I was attracted to him. A friend told me that he had been really down after a divorce, but had worked at improving himself. He'd lost a lot of weight, took some tanning sessions at a salon, and worked out at a singles gym. He was involved in practically every group in our community."

Gerald spotted Annie at a fund-raiser, and moved right in on a campaign to win her heart.

She sort of hoped he'd try to win her body, but Annie admitted that lovemaking sessions were as brief and unsatisfactory with Gerald as they had been with Harvey, although for different reasons. Harvey was in a TV-induced coma; Gerald was too busy.

"But we had a lot of fun. It was a different world for me," said Annie. For six months, the couple was a constant twosome at civic functions, political parties, and awards banquets because they were often on the committee.

"My Lord, I went to so many openings I swear I'd

probably have gone to the opening of a garage door if you'd asked me," Annie remembers.

One evening after Gerald had departed with a flurry of "Ta ta, Darling's" and a "Take care of your sweet self, I have to go home to plan my Rotary agendas for next year," Annie sank onto her sofa. A fairly introspective woman, she had the good wits to take stock of her party-animal life with Gerald.

She admitted to her best friend, "I am flat-out exhausted. One more banquet dinner or another dinky-sized paper plate of party hors d'oeuvres, and I think I'll collapse. I need rest. I need real food. I need real conversation. Hell, I need a hug."

And then Annie came to the conclusion, "I need a new man." Annie said she began to realize that Gerald, in his particular way, balked at real intimacy as strongly as Harvey had. If you keep busy chairing, coordinating, and Roberts Rules of Ordering, you don't have time for developing an in-depth relationship. Right?

It was a landmark decision for Annie. She told Gerald gently that she needed more time to herself. Between juggling Chamber of Commerce programs and planning a tourism banquet, Gerald did find the time to tell Annie he would miss her. And he probably did, for a month or two, until he found Darlene who was as strung out on organizations as he was. They went steady for six months, and were married on the stage at an economic development convention in Cleveland.

Annie was invited to a party in their home several months after the marriage. She was amused to find the living room decor consisted entirely of Gerald's and Darlene's organizations calendar with pin marks on when and where each had to appear. It gave Annie a cluster headache when she looked over their coming year, each move carefully blocked out in advance. When she realized she'd escaped just in time, the headache disappeared.

Gerald had found what he needed, an organization junkie who hadn't yet found the kitchen. Why make dinner when the hors d'oeuvres at functions served just as well?

Annie stayed home for several months and enjoyed some home-cooked meals. She caught up with what had been happening to the grandchildren, and she bought a VCR, and watched every old movie she'd missed in the past thirty-eight years. During this time she came to know herself, not as a wife or mother, but as Annie the Woman. She was so content within herself she had about decided she didn't need a man in her life.

Then friends introduced her to Mort, an insurance salesman who'd moved to Oregon from California. Mort appealed to Annie. He was sort of skinny; his cat had the mange and he didn't know where to take her, and there was a button missing on his tweed jacket.

"I think he needs me," she decided. Mort didn't realize it then, but after he'd enjoyed two dinners at Annie's, had his cat ferried to Annie's vet and the button sewn on, he took notice. In return, he took her to a genealogy study meeting, then out for Mexican food, and repaired her garage door opener, Mort was smitten, and Annie was enraptured. The couple decided theirs was a happy blend of her taking care of him and him taking care of her. They're in the mid-life heaven all of us should be.

After years of being shuffled around by Peripatetic Paul, Betty Lou knew right off what she wanted—the opportunity to put down roots with a man who would appreciate the ordinary. It took Annie some time to establish priorities, but eventually she got herself figured out.

But what about you? You may have discovered who you are, but have you paid enough attention to what you really want? Read, explore, learn, and broaden your horizons, then make a decision. No one else can make it for you.

Counseling, whether it be self-activated or with a professional, would be helpful at this point of transition. This is forever we're talking about.

If you're definitely against professional counseling—some women consider the process an invasion of privacy—then work at self-counseling. An excellent project is to keep a day-to-day diary and be totally honest in your appraisal of yourself. Am I lonely today? Am I in need of physical love and affection? Did I get up on the wrong side of the bed today? Who appealed to me and for what reasons? Who turned me off and why? Was I fragile today, or was I resilient to the problems at hand? Was I up? Or was I down for no apparent reason? What was my energy level?

After several months, go back and read your entries and determine if there is a pattern to your emotional needs. Plan your calendar by these discoveries. Make a point of doing things you really enjoy doing. Never allow yourself to be hemmed in by well-meaning friends who believe that filling up your dance card will provide emotional fulfillment.

In your self-counseling project, set short-term goals, but for heaven's sake, make them realistic. None of this "I will find Mr. Wonderful by Christmas." The very act of clarity in organizing your goals makes for clarity in other directions of your life.

Whether you counsel yourself or seek professional help, one of the most important decisions you need to make is whether you actually need a man in your life. Reta May thought she needed a man. Eighteen months after Ernie died, Reta May realized she was tired of struggling with a sprinkler that didn't work and hearing strange noises coming from her aging washing machine. She couldn't lift her console TV to take it to the repair shop and the TV man refused to make house calls.

"I need a man," she wailed. Ralph answered the call. They had attended the same church for years, and when his wife died, it was a matter of months before Ralph showed up with a wrench in his hand.

He repaired the washing machine, hauled away the TV and replaced the sprinkler handle. Then he settled down and called for a beer. Then it was an aspirin because he'd hurt his back carrying the TV. When he told Reta's grandkids to quiet down because they were interrupting his football game, Reta May woke up to the facts of life.

What she really needed was not a life's companion but a handyman. She's cruising alone now, happy in her solitude, crunching Fritos, drinking RC Colas, and watching old movies on her brand new TV.

"Pshaw," she says when friends suggest she ac-company them to the Moose Lodge and dance a few with whomever. "Ernie and I had forty-five good years. Why gamble at this stage of my life? Let me alone. I'm happy."

Reta's happier—for the moment—alone. Thank

goodness, she had enough sense to send Ralph packing.

But not all of us are Retas. We've taken time to discover who we are and what we really want, and what we really want is to cherish and be cherished. And make it soon, please.

CHAPTER 2

HERE'S LOOKING AT YOU, KID

Fine-Tuning Your Appearance

Now that you've made the decision to add men to your menu, are you ready for the next step? Don't be nervous. Or worse, don't prepare to be bored. This chapter is not entirely about beauty secrets. I'm not going to tell you that eating gelatin will make your nails grow or that applying teabags to your eyelids before a date will make your tired peepers brighter. They will, but you can find that out in any women's magazine on the supermarket rack.

Incidentally, it won't hurt to begin picking up some of those magazines to bone up on new products, new styles and makeup tricks.

This is a hardcore how-to chapter on how men like their women to look. Don't be afraid. It's going to be much easier than you think, and you're going to look *mahvalous, dahling.*

Here goes.

All women think they know exactly how they look.

"I'm a trim blonde, tint over gray, 60-ish, blue eyes, and I don't have too many liver spots on my hands." That's how Marie would describe herself if you asked her.

Marie is like many of us. She doesn't know what she really looks like because it's been a while since she seriously studied her face in a mirror. Her too-dark eyebrows are arched into a perpetual "OH" of astonishment. Her foundation, so carefully applied to her face, stops abruptly at her chin, and because the foundation and the natural skin on her neck do not match in color, her face has a disconcertingly disembodied look. And, oh yes, she hasn't stopped to notice that she hasn't looked really good in Orange Passion lipstick since she was a sun-tanned blonde in her twenties.

Let me digress for one or two paragraphs because tans have become serious stuff. Sure, we all know that tan fat is prettier than fish-white fat, and that color makes a person look healthy. But all that sun worship wasn't too good an idea for Marie because her skin now has the texture of tanned kidskin. Great for gloves, terrible for complexions.

It's been proved that too much sun worship isn't good for anyone. If you had too much sun in your youth, you might see a dermatologist about some of the miracle drugs now available. And each night, before you sleep, thank your lucky genes if you haven't developed skin cancer in your search for the "tanned rich girl" look.

In my twenty years of newspapering, one of the saddest features I ever wrote was an article on Diane, a lovely artist. Diane grew up in the Colorado mining country and loved the clear sunshine and air in her beloved mountains. When she reacher her sixties, Diane wrote to me, asking if I wanted to tell her story. I listened, then went out to interview this once-beautiful woman who, during a period of fifteen years, had had twenty-one skin cancers removed from her face, neck and shoulders. Her dermatologist attributed the skin cancers to Diane constantly exposing her fair skin to the sun. Her perfect features were marred by zig-zags of surgical scars.

"I've had as much cosmetic surgery as I can, but it will never give me back my face again," said Diane, who wanted her horror story made public.

If you simply must have that sun-kissed color, then go for it—with one of the bronzers that are on the market. With proper application, these cosmetics can give you the glow as if you'd just stepped off the plane from the Springs—Palm, of course.

Now let's get back to Marie's good points; there are many. She has nicely even features, and actually no major problems, except that she looks her sixty-one years. First Lady Barbara Bush notwithstanding, these days it's careless to look the age on your driver's license, and a sin to look any older. Don't forget Gloria Steinem's quip when someone told her she didn't look forty.

"This is what forty looks like," Gloria shot back.

To help put moisturizer back into her skin, Marie began using moisturizers to soften and temporarily ease out lines. She consulted her doctor about one of the ultra-new drugs that can help skin that has had too much sun.

Most women over 40 look better with foundation makeup and a smidgen of blusher. Cosmetologists in any large department store will help you determine exactly the right shade, and they will counsel that less is more when it comes to mid-life makeup.

An expert helped Marie select a much lighter eyebrow pencil, which miraculously softened her features. New foundation, in a golden almond shade, blended in face and neck, while subtle mascara and eyeliner highlighted her eyes.

Be willing to give up tried and true favorites. Just because you wowed the guys with Pink Camellia lipstick at the senior prom doesn't mean that Pink Camellia is still your best shade.

Dorothy saw no reason to change her makeup because she believed that basic skin colors never change. Your coloring may be basically the same as it was when you were Sweet Sixteen, but your skin tone has aged, faded a bit.

Don't despair. What has washed out or blurred can be restored with the right makeup. It's just a matter of acquiring the makeup skills you've been too busy to bother with.

It took me awhile. Quite simply, I didn't have eyes until I began using eyeliner. But even then, I didn't do it right. When I was a little kid in Luling, Texas, only trashy women wore eye makeup. Then it became acceptable, and I ended up looking like a poor version of Elizabeth Taylor playing Cleopatra.

The change came about when my daughter, Linda, a savvy kid, took a long look at me one day and said, "Mom, let's do something with you. Your features are vanishing before my very eyes."

She underplayed what I'd overplayed, overplayed what I'd underplayed, and I went to the First Citizen's Banquet that night to hear compliments of "You've never looked so good." The most pleasing thing I heard was said behind my back. One semi-friend whispered to another, "I think she's had a face lift.'

Little things mean a lot. Aileen didn't notice the little things, and probably missed out on some really big things.

A pretty, plump widow of 64, still working as a legal secretary, Aileen is attractive. Her hair is flattering in a deceptively simple style. Her makeup looks passable, but Aileen has a serious beauty flaw. What she'd called her beauty mark at 18 is now a mole at 57, and it's growing, oh, ugh, hairs.

We all know how difficult it is to make up your face with glasses on. Aileen had never gotten around to giving herself a serious look-see in a magnifying glass. Let me tell you, that any woman over 35 who doesn't use a magnifying mirror to make up her face is not presenting her best face to the public.

My friend Marian says that if you don't use a magnifying glass to make up, your best friend won't tell you what you've missed, but your worst friend will.

Hair growing out of a mole is unattractive. So is the fine-haired mustache you, in the blindness of your middle years, think is a shadow on your upper lip. And what looks to you like a straight line of eyeliner can actually look like black rick-rack to others. Magnifying mirrors don't cost much, and you'll be amazed at how many more compliments you'll deservedly get.

About compliments. Be prepared. It's not easy for some of us to smile graciously when friends blurt out, "You're looking so good today."

Immediately the Inferior Ida in us all begins to think, "If I look good today, how bad did I look yesterday?"

Send Inferior Ida packing. She's part of your past.

If you look good today, and you know how you achieved it, then you're going to look good tomorrow, and looking good is halfway to feeling good about yourself. And feeling good about yourself is infectious. Others—and we're talking members of the male sex—love to be around an attractive and confident woman.

In the 1990s, it is nearly impossible to guess a woman's correct age if she's taken care of her body and face. Technology has provided us with too many wonderful tricks, so don't feel sneaky about using every one of them.

If you're one who can afford it, and you aren't appalled by surgery, then consult a plastic surgeon about cosmetic surgery or collagen injections. But don't be too perfect. A too-tight, too-smooth face isn't nearly as attractive as one with a few laugh lines.

However, there is no such thing as a free lunch because, although cosmetic surgery has become an art, be aware that there are still risks.

I assume that you have been taking care of your interior self. Pap smears every year? How about the regular mammogram? Especially the first basic-line mammogram that can save your life?

Time out here for a story that could have been worse. Maureen had never bothered with tests, had no time for them, and she was ignoring the little lump she felt in her right breast. She was ignoring it because she had just started seeing Hank, a high school chum, who happened back into her life after he'd heard she'd been widowed.

"I was afraid I'd need breast surgery, and who wants to face a new boyfriend with something missing? she told a worried friend.

Stupid thinking, but perhaps understandable.

The friend convinced Maureen that was stupid thinking. She went to the doctor. She was lucky and the lump was non-malignant. Not all stories have such happy endings.

But take care of your interior first of all. It's impossible to be good-looking on the outside when your inside is ailing.

Are you overweight? Has your pleasingly plump became a laughable lump? Take care of it as soon as possible if you're serious about adding men to your staple diet. It is a simple fact. Men do not like fat women. Given their choice, young, old or in-between, they loathe fat.

If you've turned into a pear, an apple or, horrors, a watermelon, get shed of those extra pounds. Twenty pounds overweight? Put it in terrible perspective by imagining the twenty pounds as four five-pound pork roasts slung around your waist. If you don't get rid of that blubber, you are never going to make it to the mainstream. Even guys who are lardos themselves like slender women.

Inflated ladies, draped in caftans by Omar the Tentmaker, who go on national TV to say how really, really happy they are at killer-whale weights are just kidding themselves. They are happy because they've given up being responsible for their bodies.

No woman is really happy huffing and puffing along like Little Toot the Tugboat. No one likes having the movie seat come with you when you rise to go out and get more popcorn. No one likes being asked to watch the purses and coats while everyone else is on the dance floor.

Two true-life stories coming up:

The first appeared in a syndicated advice column. The writer, a woman, was ranting and raving against a man who had placed a notice in the personal column. He was seeking a girlfriend, but stipulated "If your stomach measurement exceeds your chest measurement, please don't apply."

The woman writing could not understand how a male could be so shortsighted as to overlook the beauty and goodness in a heavy (kind word for fat) woman.

Of course, it's not fair, but whoever told you that life is fair? It's a man's right to ask for what he wants. And what he doesn't want is a Bouncing Betty Bump.

The second story: I can certify that this one is true as I am acquainted with the man in question. He was widowed with three children.

He was upfront about what he wanted. A wife and a helpmate, a lover and a friend—all in the same body.

A lovely and gracious woman came into his office as a temporary secretary. Her face was classic, her skin was like a baby's, and she had clouds of beautiful dark hair. Her off-center wit and warm charm were so inviting, he began stopping by her desk more and more often. She had one big drawback. She outweighed him by about twenty or thirty pounds. Like many of us, she probably avoided full-length mirrors, looking only at her attractive face and hair, and never thought of herself as fat, only "fluffy." That was the term her dear dead Edgar had used to describe her. First husbands remember us as girls, and although we may fatten, they still carry the thin-girl picture in their hearts. New beaus see us as we are today.

Freda's prospective new beau did look at her full-length. Is this a glandular problem or a gluttony problem? the matter-of-fact wife seeker asked himself. Glandular, he could understand. Gluttony is ugly.

When he invited her on a family picnic, he purposely included a big box of luscious, freshly baked doughnuts.

Would she pass the taste test? Would she refuse the doughnuts or maybe eat only one for the sake of politeness.

Sorry, folks, Freda, who was nervous at meeting the family, flunked the gluttony test. She picked at the doughnuts from the moment they were put on the picnic table. Well, my dears, the Great Doughnut Gobble meant the end of Freda, and the end of the beginning of what might have been a wonderful relationship.

"If Freda's weight was a chemical imbalance or glandular or something like that, I would have tried to overlook it," said Dwight, "but a woman who has an eating problem is hiding a more serious problem. She is lacking in will power, and doesn't think much of herself. Those kinds of problems, I don't need."

Ah, but this hypercritical creep never found a wonderful woman, you are chortling. Oh, yes, he did. He

found a lovely woman who matched Freda in grace, wit
and motherly kindness. And she happened to be a trim
brunette who encouraged him to walk and work out
and become even trimmer himself. When last spotted,
the entire family was off on a hiking trip into the Cascades. He adores and is proud of his new bride.

What has happened to Freda? She's still alone,
funny, loving and charming—but fat. She still does
temp work, and in her spare time—she has plenty of
that—she teaches classes in Japanese paper art. She still
lives with her mother, who treats her like an unpaid
maid.

Freda's world is littered with cast-aside diets and
resolutions to "Get back on program . . ." interspersed
with "I'm going to see a counselor . . ." remarks. But,
of course, she never does.

It is not fair that men like slender women rather
than fat women, but it is the hard truth. So get yourself
on a program, a regular program, not one of these fad
diets where you lose a pound a day for thirty days; then
pile it right back within a week. Reduce your food
intake, but do it under a sensible plan set out by a
doctor or a nutritionist.

The big item in nutrition right now is removing the
fat factor from your diet. This may take behavior mod-
ification in your eating habits, but you'll be delighted
with the slow but steady weight loss. Exercise combined with the right diet can work wonders with a
sluggish body.

Now, I am not talking about getting yourself so
lean that you are haggard. Too many certain-age
women diet so strenuously that they give themselves

skull faces, turkey necks and tube-boobs that touch the tummy.

The Duchess of Windsor was wrong. You can be too thin. Know when to stop. Keep that slightly plump, juicy look.

The bonus? You will feel so much better when you've lost the pounds, you won't believe it's your same tired, old body.

Is your figure in order? Wonderful. Then let's get on to the rest of you, beginning at the top.

Oh, no, you aren't still wearing that too-curly poodle that made its debut in the fifties. It never looked good the first time around unless you were a pixie gamin type who wore a size four. Too-tight curls on older women look atrocious. I wish I didn't see so many of these Shirley Temples still around.

Hair is not like fine wine. It doesn't age well.

Jill, bless her heart, hadn't looked into the mirror with honesty in twenty-six years. Had she taken a look at her prom night photo with Alfred (she called him Alfie the twenty-seven years they were married), and then into the mirror, she would have realized that her light brown hair, now lightly frosted with gray, was still pouffed, flipped and sprayed into exactly the same hairdo. Only the face has changed.

Do you ever notice that the richest women have the simplest hairdos? Follow their lead. If you are on a budget, beauty schools are inexpensive and can prove satisfactory.

Scan magazines with makeovers. Find your type and go armed with photographs of how you'd like to look. Be sensible. A Princess Di you probably are not. Few of us are.

My savvy hairdresser, Sue, has a sexy but smooth shoulder-length blonde mane. She wears a size six dress and, at 44, is old enough to be a grandmother, but she looks younger than her daughter.

"Tell your ladies to keep hairdos simple enough for men to run their fingers through," Sue advised me one morning at the shampoo bowl. "Men do not like elaborate hairdos. And they hate those kinky little curls. Make yourself touchable."

She listed two more cardinal hair sins:

Hennaed hair on an older face. No, no, no.

Dyed black hair. The harsh color is perfectly awful and adds instant age. Is there a Bitsy in your life? Bitsy was a Southern Belle grown older. In her youth, her lustrous, long black hair was her most beautiful feature. Daddy liked it pulled straight back and caught with a barrette, with an Ann Miller flip on the sides. Husband Horace adored Bitsy's crowning glory.

Daddy and Horace have both joined the heavenly choir of deceased Southern gentlemen, and Bitsy's been left a bundle. Instead of doing something meaningful with her life, she spends a great deal of her money taking long cruises where she cruises for a fellow. What she finds is men who would give Daddy another heart attack, but that's another story in another chapter. We're talking hair right now.

Though Bitsy may be togged out in the most expensive cruise line clothing available, her hair hasn't made the cut from THEN to NOW.

Some black hair grays beautifully. If you're so blessed, let it go and be casually elegant in a simple style. But if your hair is a nasty brindle-cat mix of gray, black and yellow, go into a wig shop and try on lighter shades right down to ash blonde. There is a lighter shade of hair for everyone, my hairdresser told me, but don't risk the bleach bowl until you've found the shade in a wig. Then beg, borrow or buy the wig and take it to your beautician. Actually buying a wig is a good idea; you can slip into it when you're in a look-good with-no-trouble mood.

If you do buy a wig, have it styled in exactly the same style you always wear. Make sure it stays that way by storing it properly on a stand. Have you ever cringed at the sight of a wig that is flat and matted? Oh, Lord. That is a terrible sight.

Never, never wear a wig on a date. I won't even bother to list the perils. Use your imagination.

When getting your hair done professionally, have your stylist show you exactly what she's doing and how best you can duplicate the style. With practice you can be just as turned out as the granddaughter you've watched grow up with a blow dryer in one hand and a curling iron in the other.

Don't fall for that line, "Make your hair wash and wear." Wash and wear is for underwear. Mid-life hair looks better if it's smooth.

Hair soft, sleek and shiny? Is it today? Not yesterday? Fine, then let's talk style.

Do you know your style? Is your closest filled with garments bought on impulse? Or is it filled with clothes so basic you blend with the woodwork when you enter a room?

Are your clothes old? I don't mean old in years but old in style. Please throw away those gawd-awful fuch-

sia polyester pants suits. You are as young as your body
and face look, but don't go into the junior department
and buy everything that fits.

How do you find your style? Many department
stores, ranging from the pricey Nordstrom to good old
Montgomery Ward now have personal touch represen-
tatives who delight in helping you. They will work with
you to find your individual style and will help you
purchase new clothing or accessories to perk up your
existing wardrobe.

If you're terrified of personal encounters in a department store, and are still a body walking around
without a style, head for the traditional classics department.

What are the classics? They are the simple and
elegant, softly tailored styles that are sophisticated in
cut and color. These are the camel and tweed blazers,
the flannel and jersey skirts and slacks, the silk or silk
look-alike blouses that will look as good next year as
they look this year. You simply cannot go wrong with
these savvy fashions. Everyone looks good in classic
styles, which are available at all prices.

If you feel like going giddy with trendy stuff, leave
these purchases for your accessories which can be
bought on a seasonal basis. Classics can always be updated. Many experts pooh-pooh color-draping, but it
can work miracles. I'm a walking example. For a feature
article I was writing, I was color-draped.

"You are an autumn," I was told. So, because cara-
mela, camels, creams, rusts and khakis were my favorites, I kept on wearing them.

Then my wonderful daughter stepped in again,
and, because she was learning to color drape, she want-

ed to use me for a model. She and her instructor spent more than an hour, draping and undraping me before lighted mirrors.

Finally, they looked at each other and said, "She's not an autumn; she's a summer. Here are your colors," and they handed me a color-key book with fabrics in shades I'd never worn in my life.

Powder blue. Dusty pink. White instead of cream. Silver jewelry instead of gold. Charcoal black instead of "hooker" black.

As they began draping these colors around me, my face came alive. It was nothing short of miraculous.

I now have a powder blue sweater I often wear. Everytime I wear it, I am told—not how pretty the sweater is—but how good I look. That's the key, when you're complimented on how great you look, and not how gorgeous the garment is.

I still wear my old favorites, khaki, beige, browns and rust, I just wear a more flattering shade up near my face.

Men love women who smell good, but be subtle, for heaven's sake.

I remember once I was planning to fix up my dear late mother-in-law with a really nice fellow. Inadvertently, she dropped into the shop where I was working before I could make the actual introduction. He was there buying film, and after she left, he said, not realizing she was related to me, "Whooo. That perfume makes my sinuses act up."

So much for my *yenta* matchmaking plans.

My mother-in-law was wearing an excellent per fume, which shall be nameless, but she simply overdosed. Spraying cologne on the body right after a show er works wonders as the body heat keeps it working for hours. Or spray a mist; then walk right through it. You can't miss on this one.

Make sure you're wearing the perfume; don't let it wear you.

Men don't seem to like strident perfume, scents that are harsh or too "ripe." Find a light floral or sprightly scent like Anne Klein, Lauren or Norell. Poison or Opium are strong stuff for the older gentleman who remembers women smelling like his mother's flower garden.

Now, this chapter on fine tuning your appearance wasn't too bad, was it?

Before we set out on your adventure, let's do a quickie check: Is your:

(1) Interior in shape? Health the best you and medical technology can make it? Regular "lube, oil and filter" checkups will keep your body running smoothly.

(2) Makeup properly applied? I was lucky enough to have a cosmetologist for a daughter. If you do not, visit your nearest department store and ask if makeovers are available. Practically every name brand cosmetic consultant will do free or low-cost makeovers. Put yourself in their hands. However, don't be afraid to speak up if you think you're getting a tad too made up. Ask for a street makeup do, and not an evening face.

(3) Body on its way to being sleeker and healthier? Have enough will power to pass up the Häagen-Daz coffee ice cream on those downer days. Perform a bypass on the nachos with melted Velveeta? Sure I know it's difficult. Don't you think I've been there? Losing weight is tough stuff, but it's worth it.

(4) Style in shape? Have you found your personal best? Sure you have, and I'll bet it didn't cost nearly as much as you thought it would. Every wardrobe can be updated with a few smart purchases.

All set?

I loathe cliches, but allow me one right here. Be the best you can be. You'll look and feel wonderful about yourself, and a good-looking self-confident woman can attract men like the proverbial honeypot.

And that's what we're after, isn't it?

Get moving.

CHAPTER 3

WHERE THE BOYS ARE

Don't Pass Up the Guy in the Gorilla Mask

Okay, here's where we stand. You've made the decision to seek out male company, and you have a pretty good idea of what kind of relationship you want. Your appearance is so fine-tuned that your best friends are buzzing. You're feeling great, you're looking great, and you're ready to reach out and touch someone. Then Dora Doldrums comes schlepping along to tell you there's nothing to be found.

Sour Sal echoes her wail, "Well, sure, any woman can get married if she's willing to lower her sights enough."

There are Doras and Sals in all our lives. Their pillows are perpetually tearstained, and their dirges about being alone in a lonely world are woeful to hear. Their cynicism is infectious, so distance yourself from these dolls. If they're your best friend, you obviously can't zap them out of your life, but limit your encounters with Dora and Sal to coffee breaks and keep the topics to movies recently seen and grandchildren recently hugged. I have found that women who moan that there are no good men out there are not perceptive people.

These women:

(1) Are not looking in the right places.
(2) Haven't a clue what they're really looking for.
(3) Wouldn't know a good man if they found one.

When I was writing this book, one friend called to tell me, "Now, Gloria, don't get these ladies' hopes up too much. There really isn't someone out there for everyone. Some women certainly will be disappointed when Mr. Right doesn't appear by the time they've finished the last chapter."

This dear and wonderful friend is no Dora Doldrums, nor is she sour on life. She's not puffed up with self-pity, and she's correct up to a point. Maybe your idea of Mr. Right will not appear by the time you turn the last page. But here, again, we get into perceptions of just who Mr. Right is. He is, after all, what you make of him.

It's essential to keep your options open when it comes to men. If no one who fits your definition of the right man comes along, are you willing to change your definition? Men aren't cheeseburgers. You don't step up to the counter and order: "Robert Redford's looks,

Sean Connery's voice, and Henry Kissinger's brain, to go, please."

Many women, because of needs too precisely defined, have passed up a diamond in the rough and picked up a sparkling rhinestone. Sometimes we allow this to happen because, even at our age, peer or parental pressure can inject doubt into our minds.

Take Maggie, for instance. She found love among the lobsters, but she might still be searching if she hadn't opened both her eyes and her mind.

This woman is one class act at 61 years. Widowed at 57, Maggie keeps her weight down with constant exercise. Her beautiful salt and pepper hair is carefully coiffed, and her garments have a classic elegance. Maggie often thinks about how much she'd enjoy someone to "just have fun with." No heavy romance, no commitments, just a pleasant companion.

She was a college graduate with a degree in social studies, and her first husband, Roy, had been a dermatologist. So when it came to thinking of a "fun companion," Maggie was locked into the idea of what was right for her.

Her mother, who was a society matriarch in the medium-sized city in which Maggie had grown up and still lived, stoked the fires. "Marry a professional man again, dear," her mother advised. "Life will be so much easier if you stick to your own kind." It's incredible to believe that there are still mothers around like this—no matter how old their daughters. But they do exist, and Maggie's was a queen cobra.

So, from the moment she made up her mind to re-enter the mainstream, Maggie suffered from white collar paralysis. She sat around nights waiting for a knight with a degree and title to appear and carry her away on his white charger. Actually, a white Mercedes coupe was what she had in mind.

Well, horrors. No single doctor came on the market, not even a dentist. Not only was there no white charger, there was no knight, and her own nights kept getting longer and lonelier.

One sunny morning, after a particularly restless evening (the Arts & Entertainment channel can only go so far to entertain a single woman), Maggie stopped by the local fish market. Dover sole was her goal, but she discovered something much better. What Maggie found was some absolutely scintillating conversation on foreign policy—from the plumber who was fixing the live lobster tank. They talked. And they talked. And when she finally decided she'd better get the sole out of there, the plumber, who happened to be tall and graying at the temples with an outdoorsy look, asked if he might call her.

"I'll have to admit, the first thing I thought of was 'What will Mother say?'" Maggie remembers.

Imagine, a 61-year-old mother of two, grandmother of three, worrying what her mother would say about a prospective date. Daughters are like that, no matter what our age.

Her second thought was, "Why not?"

He called two days later. They went out to dinner, expanding their foreign policy conversation into such diverse topics as whether English mystery writers were more enigmatic than American ones and whether the War Between the States might have turned the other way if Lee's lieutenants had obeyed orders at Gettysburg.

Maggie now has her companion, who is also a lover and a friend. Mother has survived even though Maggie secretly believes Mother refers to Lloyd as a mechanical engineer when she tells her friends who Maggie is dating.

Whether Maggie and Lloyd will marry, who knows? For the present, they are simply enjoying each other and are packing for a Club Med vacation.

Maggie found her heart's desire because she opened her mind to options.

Helena, a more aggressive type, saw what she wanted and simply went after it.

A divorcee in her late forties, Helena lives in a small coastal community in Oregon. She is a feisty little woman and, being in the real estate business, is used to aggressively pursuing the property listings she wants. But she never thought she'd be setting her sights on and going after a man as she would a duplex!

Attending a zone hearing about some property she owned in a nearby community, Helena noticed a husky figure lounging in the back of the room. He had the cuddly look of a burly bear and the alert eyes of an eagle.

Was she intrigued? Good Lord, yes. She casually asked the person sitting next to her who was the gentleman in the cashmere sweater?

"Oh, that's our police chief," the local answered.

Helena began reconnaissance. She asked a friend in the community if the chief was married. He was not, the friend said. His name was Hal, and he was recently divorced. To all intents, he had no single girlfriend, although several divorcees had invited him to single mixers.

More and more she found reasons to be in the small community just a dozen miles up Highway 101. During a drive through the community one morning, she spotted Hal in his uniform and he was even more handsome. Late one afternoon she spied him jogging. Not particularly athletic, she borrowed her daughter's tenspeed, piled it in the back of her station wagon and waited.

Voila! The quarry was spotted, and she began a perilous and wobbly ride up toward the figure jogging down. But he gave nary a flicker. She thought of falling off her bike at his feet but was too chicken. She might injure something vital.

Despair. She dropped by the station house one morning. He was at his desk, but he did not even look up as she quizzed the receptionist about a mythical address.

Finally, Helena took a long shot. Her 17-year-old daughter sometimes baby-sat in the condo complex where Helena had discovered Hal lived. So with daughter (who was in on the plan) firmly in tow, she rang the chief's doorbell one evening.

When he answered, Helena pulled out a small sheet of paper and said, "Sherrill is baby-sitting for the first time for you, and I always like to check out her first-timers. She's the only one I have left at home." As Helena spoke, she ran her ringless left hand through her frosted blonde hair. She smiled. Helena has a killer smile and she knows it.

He smiled back. "Well, I'm a bachelor and my youngest child is 24 and living in Seattle. I think you must have the wrong address," he said.

A lively conversation on street markings followed.

It ended with the chief suggesting that the address they wanted was two blocks away and giving them directions. Naturally, the address was where Helena's friend lived.

As he saw them off, he told Helena. "When you get Sherrill settled, why don't you come back? We'll have a glass of wine."

Bingo! Helena's daughter paid an unexpected visit to her mother's in-town friend while mother went back for that glass of wine.

I can hear you groaning from here. Too good to be true, Gloria. Don't try to fool us.

I'm not. Helena and Hal were married four months after they met.

Two months after they'd met "by chance," Helena, buoyed by two glasses of Chardonnay, confessed to Hal what she'd done.

Confessions may not always be good for the soul, but in this case it worked. Far from resenting her chutzpah, he roared with laughter, especially the tale about the quivery performance. And he is forever in awe of her cleverness and his luck in snaring such an imaginative creature.

No, I am not making up those two happy-ending stories. They happened just as I have reported.

But, of course, not all endings are going to be happy. And what you must be prepared to face is that when endings are not happy, your tender feelings will be as vulnerable as they were when you were 16 and the special HE didn't call. You will hurt, but you can't let the experience wreck your chances for future relationships.

Don't be like sweet, darling Cassie who cooked her

own goose. She and her husband, Lionel, were married forty-four years. On a Sunday afternoon drive, a drunken driver broadsided the new car for which they'd saved so long. Cassie came out of the accident with a broken arm and a sprained ankle. Lionel was killed. Their daughter lived in the next state and arrived to spend several months with her mother, but eventually Cassie was ready to face the world alone. "I will be just fine," she said as she kissed her daughter goodbye at the airport.

It took Cassie several years before she spied a man she considered interesting. A plumpish and pretty woman of 64, Cassie enjoyed nothing more than bustling about her kitchen. She could be counted on for apple strudel for the lodge bake sale. When her friends were ailing, chicken and dumplings made from scratch appeared in their kitchen. When her hospital auxiliary held its annual Christmas dinner dance, Cassie was in the kitchen marshaling the food forces while everyone else danced under the sparkling silver ball. Her kitchen was hostel for the neighborhood latchkey kids and a haven for unhappy housewives hungry for Cassie's cookies and common-sense therapy.

When Burt's wife died, Cassie felt sorry for the widower. She'd known the couple through church for years even though they'd never mingled as a foursome. Soon her womanly heart began to beat a bit faster when Burt was the lay reader on certain Sundays.

So she began bombarding the poor man with food. He couldn't be expected to feed himself, could he? The poor dear.

Irish lamb stew with homemade soda biscuits was delivered to his back door one evening; two days later a chicken divan with herb rolls appeared. A brown sugar pound cake she whipped up arrived at tea time. He asked her in to share the cake and a cup of coffee. Once inside the kitchen, his late wife's kitchen, a nervous Cassie began doing what she does best. Within minutes she was making the coffee, washing the dishes in the sink, and serving the man in his own home.

Conversation was halting. The visit ended with a trembling-voiced Cassie, who knew something had badly gone awry, offering to come over and help whenever he needed her.

The offer was met with a polite but dismissive smile. His wife had been dead less than six months before. To see another woman busying herself in Thelma's kitchen was painful to Burt. It was also unnerving for him to try and make conversation on a man/woman basis. He was still grieving.

When next Cassie appeared with a pan of lasagna, he did not answer the door even though she could see him inside. The next day, a Sunday, she overheard his neighbor tell another woman, "Well, Casserole Cassie was back again yesterday." Cassie died a thousand deaths inside.

She was devastated, simply devastated. In time, her desire for male company will override the humiliation she felt at hearing herself dubbed "Casserole Cassie." For now, she has crawled into a little shell and is hiding, afraid to make a move in a man's direction.

Burt? He's keeping company with a lady whose pie dough couldn't pass Cassie's flake test, but he seems happy.

What went wrong here? Cassie was far less bold than Helena, and she lacked that lady's finesse. Until they were snug in each other's arms, Hal didn't dream Helena had romanced him by plan.

Cassie's approach, good-hearted as it was, lacked imagination, subtlety, and tact. One dish, delivered to the door, followed up by conversation during the church's coffee hour, might have turned the trick. Burt would have felt comfortable in her presence. Her frontal attack on his kitchen scared the bejeebers out of him.

Most men are intimidated about what they call "coming on too strong" basically because men like to be in control. Cassie bustling about his late wife's kitchen affronted Burt and her trying to take charge of his life frightened him.

What was the common denominator for the two successes, the denominator lacking in Cassie's mistake?

Comfortable conversation was the key. Unfortunately, it is usually left up to the woman to introduce topics in the older man/woman relationship, and the woman must be able to chatter on cue.

Maggie is a gregarious soul, and reported that she made some flip remark about missiles vs. meals over the fish counter to her plumber. Lloyd picked up on it, and the conversation was off and sparkling. Because Maggie reads constantly and is a well-rounded conversationalist, there's never been any lack of talk between the two.

Not quite as well read as Maggie, but probably more street savvy, Helena knew what to do. Once she was comfortably ensconced on the chief's sofa, she began asking him about crime statistics in his city.

On his own ground, Hal blossomed. By the time the second drink had been served, he was on his way to asking this fascinating woman out to dinner. If asked, he would have said, "She's great to talk to."

Actually, Helena didn't have to talk that much. She listened.

Good move, Helena. She planned ahead.

Maggie relied on her own intelligence and improvised.

Cassie had no backup plan. Once the brown sugar pound cake's excellence was talked out, she had no place to go—or thought she hadn't.

If she'd worked out a game plan, she would have asked shy Burt what he thought about the plans to enlarge the parish hall. Was the extra space necessary? Could the parishioners bear the financial burden? And what did he really think . . .?

A hop from this to community issues would have put them on safe conversational ground. Burt could have been comfortable and this might have been a match made in heaven.

"Why did you like me?" is a question that women often ask men. This is quickly followed by, "What made you ask me out again?'

Lord knows even the most confident of us need reassurance from our men.

One recently married man answered his wife this way:

"It was the 40 D-cups in that white sweater. They sent me into a sexual frenzy."

When he turned serious, he said, "I felt comfortable with you from the first moment. I don't talk a lot, but you kept the conversational ball bouncing. I never had time to feel awkward with you.

"And, oh God, I never felt like I had to put out

some sophisticated line. I couldn't do that when I was 25, and I sure as hell hadn't learned by the time I was 65."

D-cups not withstanding, the main attraction between this couple, who are still behaving like honeymooners, is the relaxed feeling that flows between them.

You've heard stories both happy and sad, but you're still wondering when the guy in the gorilla mask in the chapter's title is going to make his appearance. We're talking singles clubs, and dear, it's a jungle in there.

Whether to try singles clubs must be your decision. Some are grand; some are merely body exchange clubs with male members presiding over harems. You'll have to decide this one yourself, based on what's available in your particular town. Some work. Some don't. This one did.

So, now you're going to hear about one gorilla, who hung out in a particular single jungle. Caroline and her friend Anna Lee finally got up enough courage to attend a singles club meeting.

It was the group's Halloween party. Caroline dressed as a gypsy and Anna Lee went as an old-fashioned schoolmarm. In fact, Anna Lee was a schoolmarm, divorced and 40-ish. Both she and Caroline had held out against attending a Single Again meeting, but it was Halloween. Here comes the gorilla mask story.

"I felt as if I was offering myself up on a platter to single men. I've always considered singles groups the pits," Caroline said. "But what the heck? Halloween is Halloween, and we were tired of making our own candy corn to hand out to other people's grandchildren.

"We walked in, and there was this guy in the corner in a gorilla mask. When I walked over to the punch bowl, the gorilla sort of sidled over to me and made some 'Ugh, ugh, growl, growl' noises.

"I thought, Oh, Lord, give me a break. What do I do now, say 'Me Jane?' Something stopped me. So I gave him a smile and said, 'Who are you in real life?' We sort of joked about the other costumes and finally ended up entering the 'Land of a Thousand Dances' contest. He could do the Philly and the Skate better than I could. And I hadn't done The Pony since college.

"We had a great time dancing. When the time came to unmask. I nearly fainted. Here was this good-looking guy who didn't need to hide behind a gorilla mask. He's a CPA, who said he was long on figures but short on conversation, and wore the gorilla mask because he felt dumb attending a singles party. Said he felt like beef on a platter.

"I confessed by own fears. We didn't stop talking that night. The next day at work, he called and we went to a foreign film. They're his favorites. Mine, too.

"No marriage bells yet, but we're good together. We fit. And we'd never have met if I had passed up the guy in the gorilla mask."

Are you wondering what happened to Anna Lee the school teacher? Stick with me. She's coming up in the "Getting Personal" chapter, the one about answering personal ads.

So you're asking where the guys are? Everywhere. You may find one crouched behind a lobster tank with a wrench in his hand, or listening in on a land-use planning meeting, or hiding in a gorilla mask.

But you're sure not going to find one if you continue to baby-sit for your grandchildren every available evening. If you want to be in the mainstream, get into the mainstream. And I don't want to hear any whining about your not being as special as lively Maggie, clever Helena or adventuresome Caroline.

You are you, your own special self.

Here's your game plan. Pay attention and don't give me any excuses.

Give up "Masterpiece Theater." Or "Dallas." Or "As the World Turns." Make your own world turn.

If you like to read: Join a Great Books study group. Volunteer as an aide for your public library.

Are you a joiner? So you like pomp, circumstance and ritual and wearing evening gowns with silver slippers? Look into joining an Eastern Star organization. Masons and Eastern Star members work tandem when it comes to socials.

A 17-year-old in a 60-year-old body: How about a health club to make the body fit the mental age? If money is a problem, try the YMCA. Yes, they have programs for women but the M still stands for men.

Or join a community college group on ballroom dancing or folk dancing. No partners are needed, especially in the folk dance class, but you soon may find one. Community college are bonanzas for singles on a budget. They offer classes on practically everything from small business management (a great one where male enrollment is concerned) to international travel to refinishing furniture to conversational Italian. Steer clear of subjects primarily of interest to women. I mean, don't register for cake decorating in hopes of meeting a single baker. The odds are not in your favor.

Long on culture? Short on cash? Offer your body

and soul to the community theater. If you don't want to emote soulfully, they'll welcome your body for design and construction of sets, costumes, prompt actors, and handle props.

Politically savvy or want to be? Your possibilities in this line are endless. Find a candidate of your choice and work on his or her campaign. Attend community meetings on civic issues.

Chamber of Commerce groups have booster clubs who aid business folks in their activities. And more often than not, half of the business folks are men.

Don't overlook church. Today's churches offer special courses for those who have been divorced or widowed. Pastor Steve Bearden, who holds degrees in theology and in marriage and family therapy, is pastor to the singles at the First Church of the Nazarene in Salem, Oregon.

In four years, his Divorce Recovery course has drawn six hundred singles into the church, and more than one-half have remained as members, he said. Many churches in the Salem area refer their members to the Nazarene workshop on working through the pain of a divorce.

The Seventh Day Adventist Church has a wonderful dating service, Adventist Contact, where similar interests are matched. One of the most successful marriages I know resulted from an Adventist Contact encounter.

Sooner or later, you knew I was going to talk to you about single women going to bars. If you and your mate frequented bars and you feel at home in a lounge atmosphere, then by all means go to one.

I have some tips on bar manners offered by Grace

Strom, my chum who owns one of the Oregon Coast's greatest fun spots, the Sea Hag. Amazing Grace maintains you can find true happiness in a bar encounter, but she offers some safeguard advice.

The Gospel According to Gracie

— Avoid taverns. Taverns are young men's country clubs and old men's drunk tanks. There are few men in taverns who still interest a mature and thinking woman.

— If you are lucky enough to have a friend who owns or works at a lounge, visit his or her establishment. If you don't have a friend in the biz, choose a lounge that is attached to a nice restaurant. Look for one that has a lounge act or a musical group that plays for dancing. Drinking establishments without entertainment are just that—drinking establishments. Go for the fun of it.

— Once you've found a lounge in which you feel comfortable, take one friend there for dinner. Arrive about thirty minutes before the live entertainment begins.

— Do not go into bars with a pack of friends. For some gawd-awful reason, more than two women in a group sound like a pack of hyenas braying over intended prey. Sorry, ladies, it's our voices or something. And few men will ask one woman in a pack to dance. Most men are just not brave enough. They will sit and chat with one or two women, but no more.

— If a man asks you to dance and you do so, you're not obligated to spend the evening with him. If you would like more of his company, and he asks to sit a spell and buy you a drink, accept. If he smelled like stale cigarettes and leftover lasagna while you were dancing and you now "vant to be alone," say "No, thank you" like you mean it.

— If he becomes a problem, get up and leave. A well-run establishment, said Grace, has help who look after single women. You'll no doubt have a staffer at your elbow if the guy's a pest.

— DO NOT EVER LEAVE A BAR WITH A MAN YOU'VE JUST MET. NEVER, NEVER, NEVER.

However, if he's to your liking, and the evening is drawing to a close, put your hand on his arm and say, "I've enjoyed this. I hope you give me a call sometime." But don't offer your phone number unless he agrees that he, too, has enjoyed the evening.

If you are simply not comfortable in a bar and have to drink too much to have a good time, just don't go, Gracie said. She will miss you but will certainly understand.

The key to meeting men with your interests is: Be a joiner. Volunteer. Participate.

Even if you're a nine-to-five woman, leave some nights clear for giving service to others. More and more men are becoming volunteers.

This chapter could go on for pages. Consult the "Happenings" or calendar column in your local newspapers. You'll be amazed at what's going on out there.

Keep those options and your eyes open. The broader your base, the greater your possibilities.

CHAPTER 4

THE PERSONAL AD

Is It for You?

Loving, caring sharing man of 58 wants companion to share his life. Likes long walks on the beach, cuddling in front of a fire, preparing gourmet meals together, watching old movies and browsing through antique shops. Write me if you love what I love. GOM.

When Anita, a fifty-five-year-old grandmother, read this ad in a sophisticated city magazine, her heart, which had been in a deep freeze since her husband of thirty years defected to a woman younger than their daughter, began to thaw.

Anita had heard of personal ads. Her *au courant* friend, Nona, said, "Get with it, girl. So what if your grandmother told you nice ladies don't meet nice guys by advertising. Your grandmother was married fifty-five years to the same nice guy. You're young yet, you're attractive, and right now you're so hurt you're never going to recover unless some nice guy pushes all the right buttons.

When Nona left that day, she deposited several magazines and periodicals on Anita's coffee table.

"Now, read these and see what sounds good. Look at it this way. You walk into a candy store," she said, "and the bon-bons are all right in front of you. You can choose any one you like, take it home and taste it, and if you don't like it, you make another trip to the candy store."

Anita was a tick turned off by Nona's simile, but she had to admit that her friend, who was 57, led a active social life while she herself was withering on the vine. For Nona it was dinner with Eric, kite-flying on the beach with Ted, or a trip to Baja with Nathan.

Anything would beat settling down with the *Time* and *People* magazines on a Friday night. Anita tried the singles clubs, but she hadn't found one she felt comfortable with. Most had a preponderance of men who looked her over as if she was the after-dinner treat.

Yes, a change of style was definitely in order, and the loving, caring, sharing man of the ad sounded like a good place to begin.

But Anita was a novice at personal ads and she didn't know the key initials by which personal ad followers identify each other. Luckily, Nona stopped her before she wrote a warm letter of introduction to the "loving, caring, sharing" man who signed himself "GOM," which, in personal ad jargon, designates a Gay Oriental Male.

The personal ad, a mating phenomenon of the

1980s, will probably take on even greater importance in the 1990s as the number of singles increase, and they seek to enlarge their circle of friends.

Every metropolitan newspaper has a personal column, and such slick magazines as *The Washingtonian* have toney personal columns where everyone sounds like a dream come true. Personal ads run in counterculture magazines, intellectual literary magazines and your neighborhood shopper.

Some ads are specialized, according to race, with contacts in foreign countries. You'll be fascinated, perhaps appalled, by the ads stating that ladies in Asia desire traditional relationships with American men; Latin ladies want to meet single American men for love and marriage; British ladies and gentleman seek American ladies and gentleman for friendship and romance.

Don't be disheartened. If you decide against a personal ad, they still make good reading, because personal columns also offer bonuses, and you may find some worthwhile activity groups listed. Marilyn found a singles tennis tournament in a big-city magazine, signed up for the day's play, and hasn't had to write a personal ad. She's playing doubles with a nice guy named Keith. Doris hadn't ridden horseback since she was a kid in Arizona, but she was attracted by a trailriders' group in the personals of her California newspaper. Joanna had never played bridge, but the beginners' bridge group in the personal ads sounded interesting. She joined, and is deep into bridge conventions, tournaments and duplicate play.

When it comes to meeting a man, there are several reasons why a woman might turn to personal ads. She may be weary of socializing vis-à-vis; she may have exhausted the social resources in her hometown, or she may have a dash of daring in her soul and long for a taste of the unknown. If you can examine your motives and attitude about personal advertising, and still feel good about exploring the options, then go for it. Desperation is not a good motive,

But first, let's learn the language. We don't want you going for the wrong guy like Anita. Here's a crash course in personal ad lingo.

D stands for divorced. S stands for single. W stands for widowed and for white; B is for black, O or A is for Oriental or Asian, J is for Jewish. M and F are naturally male and female. BI is bi-sexual, G is gay.

Through interviews with women of ages 42 to 59, I learned the pros and cons of personal ad meeting. Here are their stories:

SUSAN: A 44-year-old reporter was assigned to do a feature story on personal ads. Being a good investigative reporter, she decided not to take the word of those who had done, but "do" herself. She inserted an ad in the personal columns of her newspaper.

Her ad read: "Lively, athletic blonde of 40-ish persuasion would like companion who is interested in hiking, racquetball, golf and running. Marriage is not my goal; companionship is."

Her newspaper is in a town of less than 100,000 with a readership of about 50,000. Within one week, Susan had thirty-two replies to her ad.

The would-be companions ranged in age from 32 to 58, and their employment was varied. There were letters from a district court judge, several attorneys, three CPAs, a sprinkling of data processors, a serving station attendant, and one dentist. Because the city was a state capital, many of the men held state jobs. Several were from outlying smaller towns, and two were from a large city fifty-five miles to the north. One came from the pressroom of Susan's own newspaper, a man with whom she had been playing racquetball off and on for a year.

She was floored by the response but set about answering the ones that most intrigued her. In the next three months, she was taken to dinner five times, played racquetball eight times, and was treated to a picnic at an area winery. She attended four movies—of her choice—and a professional basketball game.

"Actually," she said, "It was the time of my life. I never dated that much in my life, even when I was in high school and college. I enjoyed the attention."

Susan struck up lasting friendships with some of the men. Recently she was called and asked, by one of the CPAs, if she would attend dancing school with him, at his cost. He was marrying a childhood sweetheart, and he wanted to be able to dance at his wedding reception.

This was one request Susan had to refuse. She was too busy planning her own wedding. She is marrying one of the state workers, a hunky guy who is four years younger than she. "But who's counting?" asked a happier-than-ever Susan.

RUBY: This displaced homemaker of fifty-six went into the personal ad game for all the wrong reasons. She had been divorced by a husband of many years and left with little more than a house and $500-a-month alimony. She had married right out of high school and had no marketable skills except the ability to keep a nice house, say the right things at a company party, and make good apple pies. Ruby worked part-time as a teacher's aide at the local middle school, and took classes at night to perfect the typing and shorthand she had so lethargically studied while a girl in high school.

Although her work, her classes and her Sunday school class kept Ruby busy, she was lost and lonely in her big home, which she refused to sell. Another husband was the only answer to her problems, she thought, and because her small town was nearly devoid of eligible men, she placed an ad in the newspaper of the nearest large city.

Ruby wrote a grammatically correct personal ad listing her abilities, then sat back and waited for a man with charm and money to arrive and bail her out of her problems. She waited. And she waited. And there were no answers. Ever.

There were no takers because Ruby's ad sounded so desperate. It read something like this:

"Lonely, plumpish DWF in her sixties looking for love and companionship which could lead to lasting relationship. Good housekeeper, likes children, movies and is a good cook."

The incredible dullness of poor Ruby's ad may be a clue as to why Lew took off with a secretary who had nothing inside her bubble hairdo except her bubble brain. But at least the airhead made Lew laugh and feel good about himself in bed. Ruby had never expanded her horizons. Home and hearth were all she wanted, and, because she kept home and hearth very well, she felt that, as a wife, nothing more was required of her.

When there were no replies to her little ad, Ruby

went into deep depression and never wrote another personal ad again.

"Another rejection was all I didn't need," said Ruby, who has changed religions, and is now attending a fundamentalist church in a nearby city, one with a large singles group. She has gotten a roommate, a woman of her own age, and although she is still single, she does keep busy with friends made at church.

LILLIA: Lillia, a divorced woman in her late fifties, put an ad in one of her state's largest newspapers. She had several replies and answered all of them. Lillia went out to dinner with one, took a drive in the country with another, and enjoyed a Sunday brunch with a third. And then along came Al, the most charming and romantic man she had ever met.

On their first date, he brought flowers. On their second date, he brought a bottle of wine and flowers. On the third date, he proposed.

Lillia's son was suspicious of this mid-life charmer, who wore Brooks Brothers suits and drove a Mercedes, all with no visible means of employment. "But I don't work, darling. A family inheritance," he said, when Lillia asked him where he was employed.

Much to Lillia's annoyance, her son put a private investigator on Al's trail and soon found that he had several women—all wealthy—on his string.

The son confronted his mother, and demanded to know if Al had ever made a request for money. Lillia's silence told her son all he wanted to know. "Just a bit until the interest on his CD came in," she said tearfully. The "bit" was a bite of $10,000, and Lillia, on the advice of her son, refused.

So long, Al. Suddenly he had a pressing engagement on the other side of the world. "Ciao, darling. I must tend to my Australian interests," he sighed as he kissed her hand and sped off in the Mercedes.

Understandably, Lillia is torn between affection and anger at the son who didn't trust her judgment when it came to men. That rift will be healed because it's a rare mother who can't forgive a child. However, much of the anger is directed at herself for being so gullible. Lillia was so embarrassed that she wasn't able to spot a Grade A phony, she vowed to her closest friend, Mildred, that she would never mess around with personal ads again. "I'm sticking to men I know or know the same people I do," said this disenchanted and humiliated woman.

LOU-DELL: Even though this is not a pleasant little tale, it could have had a far worse ending. Lou-Dell was a feisty little redhead who'd been turning heads since she was a teenager. Her late husband, Wilbur, had adored her and lavished Lou-Dell with all that money and affections could provide. However, he was twenty years older than Lou-Dell, and when he died at age 79, Lou-Dell still had lot of living left in her, and plenty of money to do it with. After a few abortive dates with friends of friends, a lively friend persuaded her to answer some personal ads.

The ad she answered was intriguing: "Sexual, sensual man with a penchant for pleasure and travel, desires to meet warm woman with the same interests."

Well, why not? Lou-Dell thought as she quickly penned an answer. Just as quickly, she received a letter, charming in its Old World wording, appalling in its spelling. But the "sexual, sensual" man did sound fascinating.

The two agreed to meet in the poshest singles bar in their Northwest city.

Lou-Dell later told her friend "there should have been clouds parting and celestial music playing" when she caught sight of him. He was gorgeous, he was Italian, and he was about fifteen years younger than Lou-Dell. But what a charmer he turned out to be.

"Age makes no difference. It is only in the mind that it matters, *cara mio*, and I hope my being younger won't keep us apart," Tony told an enchanted Lou-Dell over cocktails.

Lou-Dell and Tony became inseparable. She displayed him like the jewel in her crown, and he danced attendance on her, ostensibly entranced by this beautiful older woman. The sex was absolutely incredible, and Lou-Dell discovered a sensual side to her nature that she never dreamed existed because good old Wilbur was a sixty-second man when it came to bed play.

Tony began to press for marriage, and Lou-Dell was tempted, but something held her back. She began to question Tony about his family. Where were they? "In Roma, my love." What are you doing in this country? "I work for my government, bella."

Truth turned out stranger than fiction in Lou-Dell's case. She was invited to visit a health club. Guess who was passing out towels and compliments to the ladies? It was Tony, who, after Lou-Dell had done some questioning of the manager, turned out to be in the U.S. on a visa and, according to the manager, he was "desperately trying to find someone to marry so he could stay in the country."

End of romance. But the experience wasn't a total loss. Lou-Dell had had a great time with Tony and had racked up some terrific memories she will never forget.

ANNA LEE: Remember the school teacher in the previous chapter? The one who went with her friend, Caroline, to a singles club Halloween party? And the friend found a winner of a fellow behind the gorilla mask?

Well, Anna Lee didn't find anyone at that party, or any of the parties that followed. So she decided to answer an ad in one of her state's most popular singles publications.

She answered an ad reading: "Academic gentleman, 40-ish, Catholic, likes good books, foreign films, art galleries on the coast, and cooking *à deux* on a rainy day."

This man sounded like the man Anna Lee had been looking for since she was widowed three years previously. Anna Lee answered the ad and found Flynn, a professor of literature at a small private college. It was the first ad Flynn had ever placed; the first ad Anna Lee ever answered.

As so they lived happily ever after. Flynn's in his fifties; Anna Lee is in her late forties. He never had children, and getting adjusted to Anna Lee's two children and three grandchildren was, as he puts it, "a learning experience."

This love affair via publication worked. Like the singles clubs. Some work. Some don't. Here are some hints from Nona, who has played the love ad game for ten years:

—Don't put your exact age if it's over forty. And don't put "mature" because many twenty-five-year-olds consider themselves mature, and we won't get into older women/younger men until the "When he's younger . . ." chapter. Simply say you're "mid-life," that can mean anything from forty to sixty-five.

A case in point was Edalene, who ran an ad stating her age as fifty-three. No answers. The same ad with "mid-life" brought in twelve replies, and she is still corresponding with two and plans to meet soon.

—Don't schedule a meeting until after you've exchanged several letters, preferably six or eight. How can you find out enough about a person in one or two letters? Perfect fools can write a respectable first letter, sometimes even two.

—When you do plan to meet, meet in a public place, and continue meeting in a public place several times. Do not divulge your address. Never get into an automobile with a man you've just met, even though you may believe you've bared your souls via the U.S. mail.

—If you get a letter from a city where you know there's a penal institution, be wary about answering. Inmates love to answer personal ads.

—If the ad you answer mentions the height but not the weight, be prepared for a plump to obese person. What isn't mentioned is just as revealing as what is.

—Make your ad as interesting as possible and mention specifics. Long walks on the beach are so plentiful, it's amazing the beaches haven't collapsed from the weight of these lovers of the sea. Don't get too esoteric. Nona once threw out names of artists and authors she adored in one of her ads. The names were so obscure, she only got one answer, and that guy had looked them up in a dictionary of little-known celebrities.

—Be honest in your appraisal of yourself. Don't say you're a "literary" sort when Danielle Steele is about as heavy a read as you're into. Don't say "athletic" if you don't want to find yourself hiking a high mountain trail with a forty five-pound backpack on your weary shoulders. If you're the mother of four hulking sons, one of whom has just presented you with your third grandchild, say so.

—Be just as honest in the needs you stipulate. Don't just write what you think a man wants to hear. You can cut through a lot of unwanted baloney and save time if you're forthright. Such ads as a "Family-loving DJW wants friendship with man who likes old movies and new restaurants," lay out your wishes, without beating around the proverbial rosebush.

—Don't pass up the blue collars in search of white collar. You may miss the chance of a lifetime. Remember Maggie and her love, Lloyd the Plumber?

—When you do agree to meet, make it a public place. Conversation is easier if drinks and dinner are involved. Discussing choices from the menu can get a good conversation started.

—Answer ads in magazines or publications that you normally read. In this way you'll find someone whose interests match your own. Unless you're prepared to travel or move, answer or place ads in publications near your home.

—Beware of the emotionally damaged soul who may drift into your life via the printed ad. Those who fantasize are fairly easy to spot; those who are out to delude are tough to get a handle on. Be careful, we're talking about your own psyche, and we don't want you to be the one who ends up emotionally damaged.

—Just as frightening are those who suffer from delusions. Nona once corresponded with a man who claimed he had invented the pantyhose machine and the kidney dialysis machine. His rambling reply was a tip-off to his mental state, and she had a sneaking suspicion he had answered every ad in the magazine.

—Most publications screen letters for direct sexual requests, although you often find men requesting women for "fun companions," a label often synonymous with playgirl or mistress. Other men openly ask for bisexual women to "increase their sexual experiences." I don't have to tell you to steer clear of these. Go into the personal ad game realizing that many men advertise for a variety of sexual partners. Never has it been so easy for a man to get sex without responsibility, and many get virtually drunk with the power of so many choices. If a guy presses for sex on the first meeting, drop him. He's not in this game for the right reasons.

—Men who request women not of their race and much younger rarely have a serious relationship in mind. They're into experimenting. Be prepared that men in their forties look for women in their twenties, men in their fifties look for women in their thirties, and many men over fifty will take anything younger if it comes in the right kind of packaging.

—Steer clear of weirdos who place ads stating that they are submissive men who desire a strict dominant partner. These guys are not after a motherly woman, who will tell them to wear their galoshes when it rains and not to forget to take out the trash when they leave.

These sickies play games you don't want to get involved in.

—If the guy writes that he wants a "discreet" relationship, that's a strong clue that he's married.

—Be aware that the competition is fierce. Arvie, a commercial airlines pilot, ran an ad in a national magazine. He got 832 replies. Arvie is in his early sixties, and is now married to Leah, a woman in her early twenties. Didn't I tell you earlier this is a buyer's market and the buyers are all men?

—If you choose to answer personal ads rather than putting one in, don't despair if the first one, two, or even more do not turn out to be winners. You really have nothing to lose but a twenty-five cent postage stamp.

—Keep your options open.

—Keep your wits about you. Rapists out on parole can answer an ad just as quickly as a single dentist.

There are no engraved-in-stone answers about whether to answer or place personal ads.

Sharon, a fiftyish tour agent, says she wouldn't dream of it. "It smacks of being desperate," she said.

Katie, a forty-four-year-old social worker, passes on the idea. Cynical Katie says, "I believe the ads are all 1's out looking for 10's."

Delores thinks personal ads are great. "Writing your own ad allows you the honesty of listing your own needs and that often takes months in regular dating routines.

"I wrote an ad stating that I had three teenage giants still at home. I figured that if a guy couldn't live with three teenage boys around the house, he wouldn't answer. I got several replies from guys who had their

own teenagers around, and one from a sexy grandfather who took me out to dinner to tell me how he
survived widowhood with three teenage kids still at
home. Tell it like is, don't spring surprises, and you
won't be disappointed."

Nona, high-energy, high-risk taker, and an IQ in
the Mensa class, loves the games, the challenge, and
the gamble.

"I haven't met a life's partner yet, but I've had a lot
of fun. A lot more than I would if I'd sat waiting on my
tuffet waiting for Prince Charming."

CHAPTER 5

LIGHTS, CAMERA, ACTION

The First Date

The first date. Lord, I remember it well. In fact, the first date was the catalyst which stirred up this book.

There I was, a loving grandmother of fifty-three, fresh out of a divorce. My choice. I was baby-sitting that Saturday morning, my grandson, Joel, crawling around the kitchen floor, heading for the dog's dish as fast as his baby hands and knees could carry him.

The phone rang.

It was a man! He was calling me for a dinner date. My first date since 1948 and that one resulted in love, marriage and three babies who now have babies of their own.

I was trying to be intelligent, witty, sexy and casual—above all casual. I didn't want this guy to know I hadn't been on a date since I was seventeen. And here's this little boy, just out of reach, devouring dog food like it was popcorn.

When I hung up I began to laugh. At that moment, I was the quintessential grandmother of the 1990s, in a situation my own grandmother would have never found herself in.

My first date. It would make a great Sunday column for the newspaper, I thought and began to make notes, but soon I realized a single grandmother entering the dating scene was too big a subject for a fifteen-inch personal column.

And so this book was born. And that's all you're going to hear about my history. You want to talk about your upcoming first date and all the other dates you're going to have.

Ten to one your first date is going to be a dinner date. Men are most comfortable asking a woman out to dinner. The entertainment is preplanned. A waiter hands you a menu. You discuss your selections. You're talking. You two have made a decision together. It is the beginning.

Should you suggest a restaurant? Not unless he asks you. There's time enough to assert your knowledge. Let him be in command.

Since we already went into fine-tuning your image, I won't tell you what to wear except to keep it simple. Unless you've been invited to a country club ball or square dance, skip the glitz or frills. Men are often put off by women who overdress. A tailored but feminine dress, a skirt, soft sweater or blouse with a blazer are all comfy clothes. These classics don't intimidate men, and we don't want to frighten the fellow, do we?

The door bell rings. It is the moment of truth.

Well, let's go back a little way. There's a bit of scene setting to do. What's he going to see when he enters your home for the first time? Of course, your living room or family room, whichever your front door opens onto, is clean. You've made sure that your scruffy but beloved slippers are back in your closet. If you must have munchies around you at all times as I do, have them in a bowl or a clever basket. No open bags of Hawaiian potato chips and a half-finished can of Dr. Pepper around. Leave those little surprises until later.

What you want to establish here is your identity, your personality. The ambience in which you live is fascinating to a man. Let him sneak a little peek of you. And let him be intrigued by what he sees.

You read don't you? Leave out the book you're reading, the bookmark plainly visible. Have your magazines, *National Enquirer* excepted, scattered about. You are what you read. What he sees will be you.

Does your home smell good? I harped about you always smelling good. Make your home smell just as good. Bake an apple pie before he gets there. If the dinner date goes well, then you can ask him back to your house for dessert. If you can't stand the guy and never want to see him again, come back and eat the pie yourself. There's nothing more comforting than mother's apple pie even if you're the mother who had to make it.

Apple pie just not your thing, but you still want

your home to smell inviting? Sort of a dirty trick for the poor guy to smell homemade pie, but a little slice of olfactory pleasure is the simmering of apple slices and spices in a pan of water.

Candles? Sweet smelling candles create a wonderful atmosphere. They're not all that expensive, and you're going to love the aroma even if the date had soured and sulked out of your life.

Have a little music on the radio or stereo when he arrives. Nothing too intrusive. No Willie Nelson and Julio Iglesio reminiscing about the girls they've known. No Bach fugue blathering. Just have some of what my oldest son calls dentist office music. You know, some of those wonderful instrumentals of all-time favorites. If you don't have the records, switch the dial. Every city has a station to romance by.

Why all this? You're a woman of the nineties! You don't need to set scenes. You're what you are, and that's that and you don't even like me suggesting you trump up a little trickery with sweet smells and sweet sounds.

Well, frankly, my dear, I meant no offense. I would hope that your home is always welcoming. Those well-meant hints are just to remind you of something you may have forgotten while living solitaire.

All right? The next step.

Be ready. Don't, as did one stupid woman I know, think you're being preciously female if your fingernails are not dry, and you're waving them helplessly in the air when he rings the doorbell.

You do want to give him the impression that you've been waiting for this evening, don't you? Even if you've had to leave work early to get the house cleaned up and yourself in top condition, do him the honor of punctuality.

However, after you've invited him in, do ask him to sit down and if you can pour him a glass of wine. If you're non-drinkers, then ask if he'd like ice tea if it's warm, perhaps iced coffee. If it's cold and chilly outside, ask if he'd like a cup of hot cider. Hint: Hot cider can make a house smell wonderful.

If you're of a crowd which begins an evening with a drink, then by all means ask if he'd like a "starter." But don't offer a second. You don't want to wind up in a ditch.

If he accepts a beverage offer, hand it to him; then leave the room to get your bag, your coat, a powder on the nose, anything to leave him alone in your room. Let him get his bearings, and get a little taste of the "you" so carefully left around.

All set? Don't do as I did, do as I say. I was always too assertive. By the time the man had walked around the car to help me get into it, I was already in it. I will never forget his face. And I never did it again.

Pause a few moments. If the jerk hops in and revs the motor, you've got your clue he's not going to open the door for you, but give him the opportunity to treat you like a lady.

If your date is a co-worker, then your conversation is off and running as you discuss the current climate in your place of business. But don't tell all you know about the office gossip, please. Of course you gossip, we all do, but don't let on right off.

If you barely know this man or it's a blind date, be prepared to make conversation. DON'T be like that legendary lady we've all heard about, the one who chirped cheerily, "Well, they picked up the garbage today."

Read current magazines and newspapers for topics. Being armed with topics can save a bundle of awkward silence. Having been a reporter for nearly twenty years when I had my First Date, conversation was easy for me. Meeting people and establishing rapport with them was a trick I'd had to learn early on in the news business. You don't get a good story if you can't get your sources to talk to you.

So try the traditional newspaper questions; the old who, what, when, where, why and how. Well, naturally, you know who he is, but you may not know who he really is. If he's a co-worker, you may know who he is from nine to five but do you know who he is when the workday is over?

A simple, "What do you do when you're not working?" sounds basic and uninteresting, but if he's a sailor, a hunter, a fisherman, a woodworker or hobbyist of any sort, he'll welcome the opportunity to tell you.

Be subtle with your questioning. To many clipped questions and you'll come off sounding as interrogative as Joe Friday.

My husband and I were introduced by mutual friends. Although I was a friend of the wife and he the longtime golf partner of the husband, we'd not known the introducing couple as a couple, we knew them as individuals.

This was an ideal situation. We had "built-in" friends to chum around without too much previous-partner togetherness. Some relationships work well if you've known each other's spouses, but I prefer there still be a bit of mystique.

Perhaps your first date won't be a simple dinner date. Perhaps it will be as complicated as was Jane's.

"George called and asked if I wanted to play golf at a fairly distant mountain resort. I adore golf, so I quickly agreed," said the seventyish widow who has the body of a thirty-five-year-old. "It sounded so wonderful. A lovely drive through the Cascades. Golf at one of Oregon's most beautiful resorts.

"And then . . ."

Well, it was the "And then . . ." that had Janie spooked. The moment she'd agreed to the date, she began to regret. She worried and she worried. She was a downright nervous wreck.

The Friday night before the Saturday date, she spent the entire night having the jitters, such a bad case that by the next morning she knew she was in no shape to go anywhere.

She called George and told him she had the flu, and she could have, so rotten did she feel. She put on her warmest fuzzy robe and took to her sofa with an old movie on her VCR.

At 10 A.M., her doorbell rang. It was George with an adorable "Get Well" care package: orange juice, soup, crackers, even some aspirins.

"I may have lied about the flu, but I certainly looked awful enough to make my sick story sound believable. He stayed awhile, we watched that old movie, the wonderful one where Deborah Kerr and Cary Grant agree to meet one year from the day. And then she gets hit by a car and he can't find her and when he does she's crippled.

"It's a wonderful love story. By the time he'd fixed me hot tea in my own kitchen, served us some soup, and we'd lived though Cary's and Deborah's tragic story with the happy ending, I was feeling very comfy with this man."

When he departed around noon to let her "get some rest" she had tender feelings for this thoughtful man. In the middle of the afternoon, she realized that their "First Date" had already happened.

He phoned later that afternoon, and several times the next week to check on her. When he called Thursday to ask if she felt like that drive to the mountain resort with maybe not strenuous golf, but just some sight seeing, she felt perfectly calm about accepting.

Yes, they did play golf and yes, they did stay the night at one of the resort's condonimiums—they were a bit tired. But no, clever Janie did not sleep with George that evening. After some warm after-dinner kisses while watching TV, she retired to the master bedroom alone.

It wasn't until the third golf date at the resort that they built a cozy fire after dinner at the lodge. When it was suggested that perhaps it was too late to start home, it was Janie who did the suggesting.

"I don't advise anyone worrying so much about a first date that they get sick, and the date turns out to be in your own living room with him serving you chicken noodle soup, but that's the way our relationship began. We still laugh about our first date," Janie said.

What should a first date be?

One word can wrap it up. Comfortable. Bet you thought the word would be exciting. Or stimulating. Or maybe even sexual.

Of course the date can be exciting. A little unpredictability on your part could make it exciting. Like

Jacqueline. She'd met her date only once before, some ten years before. When a friend asked him if he'd like a blind date with Jacqueline, Jerry said yes, but he didn't really remember what she'd looked like and he wasn't particularly excited.

But when she walked out and gave him a hug and a warm kiss (on the cheek) and "she looked so good, she smelled so good and she felt so good," he found the unexpected embrace exciting enough to make a return engagement to see what she'd do next.

Stimulating? Jacqueline read everything she could get her hands on including labels on soup cans, so there was little she couldn't talk about.

"I know a little bit about a lot of things," she laughs.

Their conversation was stimulating and Jerry was hooked by her wit.

But without the prime ingredient of any successful relationship—comfort—Jerry wouldn't have been so smitten. By the third date, he was completely relaxed and happy.

From dating grandmothers and grandfathers I've known and loved, here are some tips for the first dates and how to get a second if you so choose. Do not:

—Play verbal games. Don't expect a return engagement if you make things uncomfortable by being flippant, sarcastic, or by using bad language. Older men are not used to their women using four-letter words. Sexual innuendoes are definitely out. Men don't like to be threatened by a woman with a locker-room mouth.

—Come on too heavy with opinions on politics, religion, abortion, teen sex or any other current issue.

Sure, you've got opinions but don't try to ram them down his throat the first date. You'll never get a second chance. If he voices his own strenuously, then say quietly, "I just don't feel that way."

And don't accept another date.

–Talk too much. Some women feel they simply must fill the silence with words. Don't be afraid of silence. It doesn't kill a relationship.

–Brag about your children and grandchildren. Of course we know you love the darlings, but don't come on like the annual Christmas letter you've learned to despise. Maybe your children are at Stanford and tapped for the big time, don't go on and on, even if asked. It's boring, and anyway, how do you know your date's children aren't in such fine shape. Maybe his kid is in a drug rehabilitation center. Don't elaborate on your wonderful kids, or on the other hand, if your kids are the ones in the rehabilitation center, don't go on about that either.

–Play one-upmanship. My car is bigger than your car. My job is better than your job. My friends are bigger than your friends. Oh, Lord, there is no end to this, and all you accomplish is to drive the man away to a woman he can feel comfortable with. There's that word again.

–Don't be afraid to let on that you don't know everything about everything. You're not going to appear dumb, you're going to give the guy a chance to shine in his own field of expertise.

–Be flexible. If he changes date plans in midstream, don't fold your lips and say "No, thanks" unless it's something you positively want no part of.

Spontaneity is fun. Never ever be so inflexible you dampen a guy's spirits.

–Please, darling. Don't tell all you know about yourself. If there's a divorce, don't give the details. Don't fill him in on all your likes, dislikes and personal foibles. If he plumbs your mental depths completely the first time out, what's to look forward to?

–Don't be disappointed if you do everything right and there's no second invitation. Every first date does not lead to a lasting relationship.

DO:

–Be cheerful and full of happy expectation about the evening ahead. Don't be afraid to show appreciation.

–Touch. You don't have to do the clinging ivy routine or climb his frame while he's driving, but don't be afraid to touch, even on the first date. Like Jacqueline with her surprise greeting kiss, a warm touch can stimulate interest. And interest always brings forth another invitation.

–Everything possible to make the evening comfortable. Yes, there's that word again. It's not overkill. Comfy ease between a man and a woman can take a relationship to the heights.

Comfort can also can bring forth another invitation.

And that's what we're after here, isn't it?

CHAPTER 6

SURVIVING IN THE MARKETPLACE

As I've said before, it's a buyer's market out there, and the buyers are all men, unless you're an older version of Cher or a younger version of Barbara Hutton. But you're not afraid to compete. And despite the threatening statistic that warns a woman she is more apt to be a crime victim that she is to a bride, you're not worried. You've made up your mind that you'd rather be hugged than mugged, so look out world, here you come.

I've already told you where the boys are. You've found a passel of them but now you're a bit confused about what you've found. During the past four years, the scores of grandmothers I've interviewed offer their input and their insight as to what you may find in the marketplace.

There are some blue ribbon winners in the field of

men, and it really isn't necessary to do as my friend Marian suggests: "Catch them at the coffin or at the courthouse."

The trick is to be able to pick yourself a winner and discard the losers. It is remarkably easy for a caring and nurturing woman to become enmeshed in a relationship where the fellow is so filled with "sturm und drang," she spends far too much energy trying to make him happy. The give-and-take of happiness must be balanced in a successful alliance.

One word of advice: Don't go into a relationship believing you can recharge a loser's batteries. Once in a great while, as Georgia does in an upcoming chapter, can you make an older leopard change his spots. It's not impossible, but make sure you can live with the spots before your heart is broken and your mind bent.

From the grandmothers who have been there, here are the lovers to leave:

Hollywood Hal: At first blush, Hal is a marvelous date. How could this blossom in the garden of life go unappreciated and uncut? He's thoughtful to a fault. When you're tired of the world beating on your head, Hal is there.

He'll call your office and tell you, "Stop by. I've got something for you."

What he'll have might be a rare roast beef sandwich arranged on a silver tray, triple cream brie, crackers, and a bottle of vintage Chardonnay on ice. Vivaldi, your favorite music to unwind by, is playing softly on the stereo. Is this nice or what?

Flowers arrive with little calligraphed notes of appropriate quotes, or maybe some of Hal's original poet-

ry. Have you died and gone to heaven? This is a Grade
A Hollywood romance scenario. Before you begin planning the reception, wait a sec. Have you noticed that
Hal merely creates an illusion of casualness? His home
is a movie set. He's the star, and he's hooked on the
effect he's creating.

My friend Marian says that if a guy seems just
perfect, he isn't.

Think now. Have you ever tried to do something
for Hal? Have you tried to clean up the kitchen after one
of his culinary treats? It doesn't need cleaning up, and
he's nervous as a bug in a birdcage when you begin
bustling about on his turf.

In fact, you'll notice that he won't let you out of
his sight in his house. You don't wander about, you
are placed on his deck, on his bed or in his living
room because all his interior decor has been choreo-
graphed.

Horrors! Now that I've called your attention to it,
you have noticed that before you make love you are
encouraged to take a shower and brush your teeth. And
immediately after the last throb (Hal does make love
beautifully!), you are practically ordered to leap up so
he can straighten the covers.

Get sensible. Remember how may charming wom-
en you've seen Hal with. He is your city's eligible bachelor, and he makes a profession of it. He's a magnificent
host who really knows how to show a woman a good
time. Why not? He's had enough practice.

Take note of the fact that Hal has been single for
nearly twenty years, and his wife left him. She's married to a complete dolt now; no one can see what she
sees in him but they're perfectly happy.

Go out with Hal, the hometown version of Warren Beatty. Enjoy the perks that go with being seen on the arm of a handsome man. Relax and enjoy the attention until you catch the first glimpse of his straying toward the newest rosebud on the block, then head back to reality.

Hal can't help it. He may be:

—The consummate romantic womanizer determined to sleep with as many women as he possibly can before he wilts.

—A closet bisexual. Don't pooh-pooh the idea. You really never got much of his weekend attention, did you? Were there times he sort of disappeared? Had to fly to another city for business? What better way to disguise homosexuality than to get the reputation for being a lady's man?

—Totally detached from a real relationship with a real woman. He goes through his routines, viewing himself, his charm and his attention, from some distant plane where he cannot really be touched. He doesn't want a relationship, he wants the starring role. You're only the bit player.

Limelight Lou: This would-be star is a stunner. He's handsome, he's talented, and he's romantic. Dating Lou is like hitting Spago's with Don Johnson. He's an instant hit with all the women. He zips from blossom to blossom, sipping a little nectar here, nibbling on an ear there.

Will he entertain? Of course, he just happened to have brought his sheet music along with him. One chorus of "Some Enchanted Evening"? Delighted. He'll give the crowd three and exit smiling. How about his imitation of a gargling fish? A horny parakeet? Lou'll do'll. Mr. Show Biz is onstage constantly.

But for some reason, the other guys don't like Lou. The words "jerk," "fool" and "numb-nuts" begin to reach your ear. He's not really successful in his high profile job either, and he doesn't have much credibility in the community. His jobs seem to change every six months to a year. He's constantly on the brink of a new beginning. He hints darkly that there is "someone out to get me." How could they? He's such a charmer. Or is he?

Lou isn't really tolerable except for short commercial breaks. He's the sizzle without the steak.

The saddest thing about Lou is that deep down he knows he's ineffectual; hence all the hullabaloo that surrounds his arrivals and departures. He's a frightened, terrified rabbit. Life hasn't been all that great for him, a series of fantastic starts and lousy finishes. He dates many woman but rarely has a lasting relationship because he doesn't understand what a loving relationship is all about.

Lou was a child of indifference. His parents weren't mean to him they just didn't pay much attention to him. Now, he's making up for it now with his dazzling life-of-the-party facade. Lou is unhappy, and he's insecure. That's why he is constantly trying to prove himself.

Unless you want to sign on as a permanent cheering squad of one, don't get attached to Lou. You want a life's partner, not another child.

Moody Max: He's the dramatist. You think Lime-

light Lou believes the world is out to get him? He's
nothing compared to Max. Intensity is this man's middle name, and crazy-making is his game.

Sure he's been married a couple of times. Want to
know what happened to those marriages? Don't bother
to ask. Max will tell you: "Women are no damn good.
They're all after one thing." It's never quite clear what
the one thing is. Max joined singles clubs and rarely
mixes. He broods in a corner and waits for some blossom to come close and try to charm him out of the
blues.

Before she knows it, she's hooked on the drama of
the entire thing. He's suing his ex-boss because the fool
couldn't see that Max was really the star of the show
and should have been given his more authority.

The locks on his door have been changed because
ex-girlfriends, not to mention ex-wives, are trying to
break down the doors and spirit away some important
papers. You never discover what important papers they
are, but you'll find yourself defending them to the
death (of the relationship). Is this man an ex-CIA agent?
He'll try to convince you that he is. Emotions are always
on the surface with Moody. Life is either beating him
down or lifting him up, it's a constant battle, and he'd
really like you to fight against the forces with him.

Max is caught in a world of duality. Everything in
his demented domain is black or white. There are no
calming shades of gray. He'll tell you that life is an up
and down, a massive plot against mankind, Toots.
What your common sense should tell you is that here's
a manic-depressive about to explode.

Don't be drawn into Max's drama. You don't need
theater to prove you're alive. Don't become a co-

dependent to Max's moods. Run, don't walk out of his life. If you hang around, you'll become his fall girl, and it will be your fault when he fails. Max may start hitting on you when life is beating him down.

Fragile Fred: He's such a dear. The big bucks babes in New York City call the Fred-types their "walkers." They are exquisite companions; they'll walk with you anywhere. And fun, Fred is a hoot to be with. His wit is deadly and devastating. He's just like another girl-friend, always ready to dish the dirt or play a prank.

Fred's always lived with his mother because it's cheaper, can't you see? Besides she needs him. He's all she's got, what with that ungrateful older brother mar-ried with those dreadful children and living in Pas-adena. Where else could Mother turn?

His job is good, his future safe. He's a heck of a good CPA. His sense of style is impeccable, and if you need advice on hairdos, evening gowns or buying a fur, Fred always knows the right places.

He is fun, just like all the Freds of this world. They're the type of man a woman doesn't want to be without. They're better companions than the best girl-friends, and they aren't jealous of the other men you're dating. Perhaps, they're a tad jealous of you for being able to date men, but that's never talked about.

Is Fred a closet queen? Don't embarrass him by asking; he may not know himself. Invite Fred as an escort, enjoy his company, and always keep Fred as a friend. So what if he reminds you of Pee-wee Herman? Pee-wee's adorable.

However, don't make any long-term commitments with Fred. If you by any chance get a proposal out of

Fred, it is probably because Mother croaked and he needs a replacement.

Crybaby Craig: Oh, goodness. He looks hard on the outside, but inside he's just a marshmallow. He may be one of the most common weeds in the singles garden.

Usually spotted while holding a drink, Craig is an intelligent guy, has a good job and is involved in civic and community affairs. You're going to find him at political parties, business mixers and single parties.

His method is always the same. He'll dance you around and listen awhile. When you ask a question about his life, Pow! he'll pounce.

By the time you've heard how much he really loved that woman, will always love that woman, and did right by that woman, you'll be gasping for air. But you can't escape because he doesn't draw a breath. Every sentence is overrun with yet another whine. Pretty soon, you'll begin to see tears forming in the corners of his eyes. He'll take another gulp of the bourbon and branch, and a sob will gurgle down low in his throat.

He tried, Lord knows he tried. He was a good husband, took out the trash, unstopped the toilets, and always carried in the groceries. His favorite statement is, "I didn't even know our marriage was in trouble. We never really had a fight. Then I came home and found out she'd run away with the guy who sold us our water softener."

"I don't know. I just don't know." Sob. Gurgle. Gulp.

"I just don't see how I'll ever love another woman," Crybaby wails as he looks to you to mend his broken heart, cure him of incipient alcoholism and balance his checkbook.

Oh dear. Life is just too much for Crybaby. You may love him enough to help, love him enough to be his boss/wife/mother/nurse, but make sure you know exactly what you're getting into. Women don't run off with the water softener salesman unless they feel short-changed at home.

Donald Dull: He's sooooo boring. There are many Donald Dulls to be found. They are really nice guys, don't have any outstanding bad habits. They are simply monotonous. Of course, if you've lived with a Moody Max, you may find Donald is just exactly what you need. So I won't say any more.

Have you found someone you're still in the dark about? Is he really as nice as he seems? Or is his good behavior a courtship ritual and a cover up for a real tyrant or maybe even a nutcase?

The grandmothers I interviewed came up with this little quiz to see if you're running to these problems, and if you are, what are you going to do about them.

Danger signals. Does he:

—Have opinions—usually negative—on prac-tically everything? Watch out. If his is the only opinion that is valid, he's not going to respect your opinion on anything that is contrary to his hide-bound ideas.

—Put you on the defensive? I'm not talking about some give-and-take on a particular subject, one where you have to get your brain in gear to prove your point. That's fun. I mean, is the man a bully? There's some-thing about a man who maneuvers a woman into feeling guilty, silly, or stupid. These guys make lousy husbands.

—Treat your family with consideration: Try this, as did one grandmother. Arrange for your grandchildren to be visiting when he comes for dinner some night. Dinner with the children, especially if one grandkid is two years old, generally separates the man from the boys you need to avoid.

—Consult you on little things: Or does he try to be the Big Boss and treat you like you're just the pretty little lady who doesn't really know quite what to do?

I have the guarantee of a married friend that the pretense of not wanting control will vanish on the wedding night, and he will become a Neo-Nazi dominating man you wish you'd never met. She's debating divorce court right now, and she's brokenhearted because she loves him. She just doesn't like him.

—React sensitively to your concerns, fears or feelings? One woman I met instantly rejected the town's best prospect because he went out of his way to run over an opossum in the road. She said he roared, "Kill the little bugger," as he put the pedal to the metal. When he called the next time, she said, "No, thank you," and told him why. He's still shaking his head at what he calls her "wimpy" behavior.

—Dress weirdly? I don't mean clinging to his cuddly old sweater, the one with the holes in the sleeves. Or bemoaning the loss of the tennis shoes that should have been tossed years ago. I'm talking about the guy who's a school crossing guard and wears his crossing guard hat to the senior dances.

Look at Howie at the senior social. He and Annette tangoed their way to love and lust, but the giant ring of keys on Howie's belt kept coming between them. It's sad but true that Howie's keys are the symbol of his manhood and the authority he once had as a custodian for a factory.

Chartreuse leisure suits, gold chains and mutton chop sideburns don't make for a mainstream lover either. The poor guy is reliving the past, and the present has no interest for him.

There's something pathetic, even creepy about guys who dress peculiarly.

—Behave cheaply on a date? If the guy is on a fixed income, don't be crass enough to knock him if he watches his pennies. I'm talking about the type of guy Margaret finally had to give up on. He owned a chain of twelve service stations, drove a Mercedes, and belonged to a country club with a triple-digit entry fee. But he and Margaret never went out to dinner unless he could find a "two-fer" coupon in the shopper or the newspaper. There's careful with money, frugal with money, and just plain cheap. A cheap boyfriend will be an even cheaper husband.

Throwing money around is an equally big turn-off for many women. I know a guy who, once he has a lady out to dinner, keeps riffling the bills in his wallet so she won't miss noticing that they are all $100s.

—Have temper tantrums? Does he turn manic in a minor traffic gridlock? Curse obscenely when passed or cut in on the road? Many men can't take traffic problems, but there's a limit to acceptable impatience.

—Like his booze? One martini and he's a riot? Two and he's surly? Three and he'll fight anyone in the bar? This is a danger signal.

—Have different values and morals? Does he tell

ethnic jokes that make you cringe? Turn any remark
into a sexual innuendo? Refer to women in crude and
uncomplimentary terms? Head for home.

—Smoke, and you loathe the smell, the taste and
the mess? Reforming an old smoker is nigh impossible
unless the old smoker wants to quit.

Does this quiz sound too tough? Are you saying to
yourself, "Well, no one is perfect. I could live with some
of those traits. And besides, he does this or that because . . ." Suddenly you find yourself making excuses
for him.

Whoa! Don't be too quick to compromise your own
self. Funny quirks have a way of becoming big issues
when you live with them every day of your life. Knowing why a guy has an unpleasant trait doesn't make
those things easier to live with.

Now, now, don't sulk on me. You're in despair
because I presented a list of crazy-makers and your
special "he" was on the list. Don't be. There are more
guys to choose from than whiners, creepers, braggarts
and dominators. I promise to give you some good guy
news now.

There are plenty of wonderful guys out there. I told
you where they are in Chapter III, and you've probably
thought of places I didn't even know to look. So, re-
evaluate the guy who has more than one of the unpleasant traits I've listed. You are not desperate, lady. You
don't have to make major compromises, just minor
negotiations.

Lucky-in-love grandmothers I have interviewed offer the following hints on the really good guys. These
winners:

—Have hobbies, but don't pursue them to excess. Golf is great and will keep him in shape for you, but if he plays eighteen holes six days a week and twenty-seven on Sundays, you may find yourself a golf widow.

Also, older men taking on younger men sports are scary, especially if you can tell the pursuit is an all-out fight against age. Sure, stories of guys 70-plus taking up downhill racing make for good reading, but such obsessive behavior may not make for good relationships.

—Know what's going on around them. They can quote the stock market's up and downs, who's who on political first base, and what the day's hot news is. They are observant, but not unnaturally curious.

—Keep themselves physically in shape. Wimpy bodies make wimpy lovers, and even if your date is not Arnold Schwarzenegger hunky, the fact that he exercises in some way is a sign of a balanced personality.

As long as we're talking about bodies, let's talk about fat. I rail against women gaining weight, and I'll rail just as loud about obese men. To me, gross overweight denotes a character imbalance, a failure of self-will, and a lack of self-respect.

—Keep themselves clean. Sorry, I have to bring this up, some men don't bathe as often as they should. A good guy does and he smells so good all the time, whether the scent is Brut, Old Spice, or plain old Ivory soap. A clean man is fun to touch. The alternative is simply awful.

If you do find a diamond in the rough, don't be afraid to suggest a shower. Perhaps à deux, it could be fun. When you're out, tell him, show him, how nice it is to get cuddly with a sweet-smelling sweetie.

—Have a good sense of humor. Having a humorous outlook on the human comedy and being able to laugh at himself are top requirements on almost any intelligent woman's list. If a woman doesn't value this quality as high, she should look for a guy who is serious without letup. One with wit, one without is a terrible combination.

—Will listen as well as talk. They'll ask questions about how you feel, what you like and your opinion is. Men of the "Me, Myself and I" persuasion are emotionally stingy and not worth fooling with.

—Have good friends. I don't mean the kind of friends who take precedence over the woman in their lives, friends who try to lure a guy out to a tavern and away from a wife or girlfriend. The buddy/buddy system can be carried to extreme. But, if you're lucky enough to find a guy who is respected by his peers, give him your best shot. He's most often a keeper.

Pay attention to this list of danger signals and good guys, and don't be too unhappy if I have taken a potshot at what, for you, might be a relationship made in heaven. Perhaps it is; perhaps you CAN take a lemon and make lemonade. If you can, more power to you.

But I don't want you to take a misstep, fall, and then cry out, "But, Gloria, you should have warned me."

I'm on your side, remember? And if a word of caution makes you think twice before committing your body and soul, then I'd rather be guilty of cynicism than of omission.

CHAPTER 7

SEX? AT OUR AGE?

You'll Be Surprised!

The time will come, much sooner than you imagine, when your sweetheart makes his move. The rules have changed since you smooched in the backseat of the 1938 Ford convertible, so be prepared.

The men who were the boys easily put off with a cuddle and a feel now want and expect the real thing. These guys want to go all the way because they know all about the sexual revolution and they want what they believe is their rightful share of the fun.

And because you are no longer a virginal teenage girl taught to sublimate all feelings physical until the ring was on the finger, you will be amazed at how much you long to touch and be touched.

Bodies wither away without physical caresses because it is a scientific fact that skin hungers for the touch of other skin.

I know, I know, there was a time after the divorce, after the funeral, when you went numb as a woman. Feminist beliefs to the contrary, most women at any age need more than a hunk to keep them happy. We are thinking creatures and a lot of thought goes into a physical relationship. No longer are we teenagers with hormones in overdrive, so the decision to take off our clothes and climb into bed with a near-stranger at this stage of our lives takes time and takes courage.

In the following chapter, we'll discuss sex with the imperfect stranger. But right now, let's just talk about the decisions that go into having sex. I hate that term. Let's call it making love. If you're just having sex, it's not going to mean anything and I want you to have everything.

But first we have to ascertain who you are.

Are you the Leaver? If you have left your mate for any reason, you are probably much more healthy mentally than a woman who has been left. The leavers have demonstrated enough character to extricate themselves from a bad situation and get on with their lives. But the Left Alones are burdened with a tremendous feeling of rejection, low self-esteem and frustration.

Unhappily, this burden can cause an imbalance of values. Well, let me tell you about Luanna. You'll weep for her, but her lesson is to be learned.

Louis, her mate of thirty-five years, calmly announced one morning that he had fallen in love with his secretary. Would you believe anything so tackily trite? Well, it happens every day and we all realize it.

Anyway, Louis took off, leaving Luanna everything but self-respect. She went temporarily insane. This attractive plumpish blonde of 47 joined every singles club in town and did everything but dance nude on tabletops with a lampshade on her head. Somebody loves me, her outrageous behavior proclaimed to the world. Pretty soon, the somebody became everybody, including Louis's best friend, who stopped by one day to fix Luanna's Weed-Eater. He became a fixture; his wife, who had been Luanna's friend, became enraged and Luanna's reputation was zilch in her own hometown.

And what had she accomplished? Absolutely nothing.

When she awoke after a night of bad sex, she still felt unloved and unrespected in addition to being burdened with guilt and self-loathing at what she had become. Promiscuity to regain self-esteem is never the answer. Luanna has moved to another town and is beginning life all over again.

If you are in the widowed state, you are sensible enough to realize that death is a natural conclusion to life and your time with that mate is over. But, it will take you time to work out your anger and frustration at being left, because in a sense you have been left, and you are just as alone as Luanna.

Here are important questions to ask yourself before you begin any physical relationship.

(1) If this relationship does not work out, am I strong enough to leave or be left again?

(2) What do I want out of this relationship?

Am I:

(A) Climbing into bed with Ted because I want physical enjoyment?

(B) Climbing into bed with Ted because I want to be held? Sex really doesn't mean that much, but I need to be cuddled.

(C) Climbing into bed with Ted because I am in love with him, and by sharing myself with him I can make him love and marry me?

(D) Going to respect myself in the morning?

There are no grades to this quiz because there are no "right" answers. You, and you alone, are mistress of your fate and you can do anything you darn well want. But it helps to know thyself and if thy can live with thyself beyond the moment.

Okay, lecture's over. I just didn't want you getting into a situation you are not emotionally ready to handle.

What we want for you is an intimate relationship in which you feel warm, comfortable and cherished. What we want for him is for you to give him the warmth, comfort and affection that allows him the freedom in which to enjoy his closeness with you.

Sex is threatening to men of any age. They may want it more than anything else—at that particular moment—but the fear of failure looms more heavily the older a man gets.

It is up to you to set the scene. You are in control.

When you meet a man whom you are really enamored with and feel comfortable with, adopt a warm and affectionate manner with him. I do not mean throw yourself at his feet. Be a flirt, but don't be a tease. Remember the girl teases of your youth? With a pout on her lips and a hand on his thigh, she promised what she rarely delivered.

You're a mature woman, too old for that silliness and that cuteness. You don't want that and neither does the man of your choice. Maybe he thinks he does, but he doesn't. Women who come on strong to older men terrify them.

What I am advising is the well-meant affectionate hug and pat that tells him "I find you very attractive and I am right here, supporting you."

You may run into a problem because some men have not been programmed to deliver physical caresses unless it precedes a lovemaking session. They can't help themselves, poor little guys. They just never got their fair share of hugs from their mothers and their dads. Physical affection was not known in their early homelife.

Like the story of Georgia and Ernie. She was a bubbly Southern Belle; Ernie was a second generation Norwegian. They met in Flagstaff, Arizona, of all unlikely places, and the mental attraction was instant. His dry droll humor fascinated her; effervescent "you all's" and giggles made him feel like a kid again.

Georgia was a toucher. When they began to date, she would always have her hand on his arm, or massage the back of his neck as he drove, or held his hand when they walked down the street.

Like a giant cat, he loved it. He confessed later that he adored being touched. But he never touched back. He literally did not know how.

Eventually, both knew that they wanted to make love to each other, but Georgia held back.

"I want to be touched because he likes to touch me,

not because he wants to make love. Doesn't he understand that?"

No, he did not, and it was not until she explained
to him her reluctance to enter into a physical relationship that represented only sex, did he understand.

And he said what were the two most important
words he ever uttered. Because he loved her and wanted to be with her for the rest of his life, he said, "Teach
me."

And she did.

So they began, and they are two of the happiest
people I have ever seen. She is in her late fifties, he is in
his early sixties and their sex life is loving, laughing and
often.

Through open communication, Georgia and Ernie
have put into action the three most important ingre-
dients in a sexual relationship.

They are:

(1) Natural warmth and affection
(2) Mutual trust
(3) Willingness to give and receive

Let's elaborate.

The first is so obvious, it seems ridiculous to state,
but natural warmth and affection is not always easy
for some to give. Georgia realized that, and was able
to communicate her love for Ernie through action and
talk.

She treasures Ernie's comment that "I never wanted to touch anybody, really touch anybody until I met
you. You made it natural and easy." It had taken this
product of a cold and reserved home many years to

realize that love should be natural and easy, and does not have to lead to sex. So it is never too late to learn the pure joy of a warm and affectionate relationship.

Not all stories are happy. Some budding romances never get off the ground and into the bed because of bad timing.

Lucilla liked Don. He was mentally her equal, financially her superior (always a nice match, ladies), and very, very eligible.

Their first date was dinner out and went very well, the conversation ping-ponged and never stopped bouncing. It was a delight for Lucilla, just coming out of a six months relationship with a man who never picked up a book from one year to the next.

The second invitation came in the form of a suggestion to have a picnic. Did she know of a good place? Why not my place, said Lucilla, who had a lovely country home.

Great idea, Don said, and at the appointed time pulled up with portable broiler, chateaubriand and French wine. And his bottle of Russian vodka.

They carried drinks as Lucilla gave him a walking tour of the property, he had another while she prepared the salad; then had two more while he grilled the steaks.

As he put the steaks down on the counter, he said, "What a pity I can't eat these."

And lurched to her sofa and collapsed.

One, two hours passed and the ZZZZZZs were still filling the air in the living room. She finally fixed a cold steak sandwich and drank a Dr. Pepper. So much for her beautifully arranged table and delicious salad.

At 11 P.M., she checked. Sleeping but not comatose he was, so she decided she'd simply go to bed with a good book. And she did.

It was about 1 A.M. when the door to Lucilla's bedroom opened, and a hairy body pounced and began making waves in her waterbed.

"Bet you thought Old Donnie was going to be out the whole night," breathed Old Vodka Breath, sticking a tongue in her ear.

In a flash, Lucilla rebounded out of the bed and asked, "Are you strong enough to drive home?"

"I don't think so," said OVB weakly.

"Then I'll have to drive you and bring your car in again tomorrow," said a determined Lucilla, looming over the bed like an avenging angel.

At the thought of someone else driving his shiny new BMW Boy Toy, Old Don made a rapid recovery, butterfly-stroked his way out of the bed and picked up his portable broiler.

Lucilla waved goodbye to him at 2 A.M. and sank happily alone back into her comforting waveless water bed. That was the last time she saw him and couldn't care less.

Well, actually, she could care less. She cared a lot, she found him interesting and attractive, but his behavior was less than attractive. And who wants a man with Stolichnaya breath anyhow?

Perhaps there could have been more for this couple, but bad timing and bad manners spoiled it all.

Let's talk about bodies.

"How can I think of getting into bed with a man?"

asked Peg, a delight of a dumpling. "I have a 60-year-old body. I'm not Dinah Shore, you know. I have a tummy bulge and some cottage cheese on my thigh, and my bosoms haven't perked in years.

"How can I possibly take off my clothes in front of a man?" she wails. It is obvious she has not found a man with whom she'd like to disrobe.

First off, let me lull fears. Unless a man has a terrible mental disorder and can only make it in bed with long-haired hard bodies (Translation: Women one-half or one-third his age), then bodies don't matter.

"If you take time to become soul mates, who looks at bodies?" my friend Marian asks.

It is true. If there are sparks, there will be fire.

And when it happens, you are simply not going to believe your reaction.

"I thought that part of my life was all over. I never thought I'd feel this way again. I get tingly when he touches me and I can't keep my hands off him. I feel like I'm 18 again," Andrea reports.

Andrea is 72, and Ron, the object of her affections, is 75.

Ron had been widowed more than a year when he was introduced to Andrea through mutual friends in Palm Desert.

The day after they met, Andrea told her friend, "I think I like him. What should I do about it?"

"Get busy before the local casserole set goes into action. I know the Portland hot dishes have been coming his way since the funeral," advised the friend, wise in the ways of widower's opportunities.

Andrea made her plans. She had been invited to a cocktail party, so she called Ron and pleaded fear of crowds. Would he . . .?

Yes, he would be delighted, he said, to accompany her to the late afternoon party.

After the party, Ron suggested dinner. She would be delighted, she said.

During the next two weeks, they took long drives, attended parties, dined out, played golf and sometime within the time span culminated their friendship with a long and loving afternoon spent between the sheets.

One month later, when Ron's car rolled out of the desert to head home to Portland, Andrea was in the passenger's seat. Just a visit to see where he lived, was the plan. She would soon return to her apartment and friends in Los Angeles.

Andrea won't tell how many stops they made on the way home; she just smiles. Now Ron, the tall and handsome quintessential gentleman, and Andrea, petite, blonde and pretty, are a couple.

Unfortunately, Andrea's settlement makes it financially expedient for her not to marry. But this has not stopped the wild-for-each-other couple. The visit has lengthened into months. Andrea has given up her apartment in Los Angeles and moved into Ron's home and social life in Oregon. Friends adore the fun-loving couple who have more invitations than they can accept.

But friends know better than to just drop by for a casual mid-afternoon visit. Ron and Andrea love their afternooners, so friends call first!

A recent headline read: IF YOU THINK YOU ARE OLD, YOU ARE. It's true.

Take Aileen. Lord, what a pistol she is. I'm sure

Guy's wife wishes someone would take Aileen, three times married, three times widowed.

The wife recently called Aileen's sister-in-law.

"Will you please tell your sister-in-law to lay off my husband," the irate wife yelled.

"Good heavens, what is she doing?" queried the puzzled relative, almost afraid to know. She's known Aileen a long time.

"She's playing kissy-face with my husband in the parking lot every night after diner. Tell her to stop breaking up my marriage!"

Well, honey, Aileen is 86 and the husband is a speedy 91. And they all live in a retirement home.

Aileen hasn't a clue that she's old, therefore, she isn't. I'm sorry about the unhappy wife, but I sort of like Aileen like she is, still sexually come-hither and no plans to slow it down.

Sexual attraction and satisfaction knows no age boundaries.

CHAPTER 8

DOING IT

New Games, New Rules

It has happened. Some way or other, some time or other, you and your honey have consummated your relationship. The deed may have been done in your home, his home, or perhaps a cozy weekend for two at a romantic hideaway.

There was no way I could have told you how to achieve this first time. That was up to you two and is none of my business. All I could do was help you set the stage and the climate for intimacy in the "Sex? At Our Age?" chapter.

If the earth moved for your first time together, wonderful. But if your first real togetherness was a dismal flop, not to worry. Not that you are worrying about it, anyway. Women are marvels at taking things in their stride, adopting a quasi-Scarlett tomorrow's-another-day approach to life in general.

Men however are different. The act of love to them is a three balls, two strikes, and no more ups in the bottom of the ninth situation. They strike out and the ball game is all over. Poor darlings.

Remember my theory that women are like twenty thousand years more evolved than men? Our advanced evolution gives us a more sensitive and thoughtful approach to life in general. If things didn't quite work out well in bed that first time, a woman knows that they will eventually. You know it's going to be all right unless you're a real mid-life sturm-und-drang bitch who rails against the flop and torments him with non-production. You do this, sweetie, and he'll be out of your life before he's barely in.

No, your mission in life, because you love him, is to take away the worry. Men at any age are sensitive about their bodies; at an older age they are tremendously vulnerable. It is up to you to build up their ego.

Forget all that feminist baloney about demanding your sexual rights in bed. Use your common sense. No woman can command a flaccid penis to perform.

As my friend Marian always says, "A man with a wilted willie is a man who's failed the self-proof test. And he needs love, dearie, lots of love."

More about problem areas later.

If your first time was easy, no doubt the second, third and maybe the fourth time was, too. You're rolling on a marvelous momentum of newness and delight. There are romantic feelings and wishes for a happy future to carry you through.

But then, reality sets in. We're grownups together. Of course, you remember how it was in your marriage. You went to bed knowing you were going to make love. He'd given the signal known only to you, and you showered, brushed your teeth and put on a pretty nightie or left off a pretty nightie, according to Herbert's preference.

Then you hopped into bed. Herbert turned off the light and hopped into bed. And then you did it. Probably the same way you'd been doing it for years.

And that was that. Afterward, you discussed the daughter's upcoming grandchild, the IRS growling for more, more, more, or the fact that the light bulb was burned out in the utility room.

Post-coital cuddling is rare in a marriage of many years. It's not because the couple doesn't love each other, they are just so used to each other it seems unnecessary.

But you and your new love are just that—new. And there should be cuddling, lots of it. Lots of appreciative pats, and hugs and kisses both little and big. You just don't keep a relationship going by giving or getting a look and hopping into bed.

You're saying, "Who didn't keep a relationship going? We kept a marriage going, didn't we?"

Did you? Or did Herbert leave you for a cutie who was not so predictable? Ouch, that hurt, didn't it? Well, only for a little while until you learn new games, new tricks.

Maybe Herbert didn't leave you for an untried filly. Maybe Herbert died. And you miss him dreadfully and nights are long and painful because he is no longer filling up that space next to you in the bed. The night is very quiet without the shake, rattle and rolls of his melodious snores and titanic turnovers.

You miss him, you miss that body. He knows that, wherever he is.

But you are one of the lucky ones. You have another man to love and cherish. Let's make it count.

Many women of our age simply don't think in terms of being a sexual and sensuous woman. We just haven't had time for it. There were the hot months of our first marriage, then the babies started coming. Marian always says that if a couple puts one bean into a jar for everytime they do it the first year they are married, then begin taking out one bean everytime they did it in the next five years, they will still have beans left in the jar. She may be right. She usually is.

There are no more colicky babies who wail in the night, no more of that mind and body-boggling fatigue that besets a younger woman trying to juggle marriage, a job and children. There are no "when" limits in our lives. Make love any time you darn well want to. Two o'clock in the afternoon is a delicious time of day to cuddle and love.

Cultivate the sensuous part of you, the woman. Begin thinking of making love. Dress for love. If you want him to touch you, make your body accessible. Don't wear clothes around the house that will in any way keep him from copping a feel. You'll enjoy the love pats as much as he will enjoy giving them.

You may think it's too late to "Think Sex." Don't you believe it!

Ready to begin enriching your love life?

First off, get rid of all the old nighties and undies that should have been retired years ago. If you must save them, wear them when you have nights alone. Let's hope you don't wear them often.

Remember Peg, the dumpling delight of "Sex? At Our Age?" And she said, "How can I take off my clothes in front of a man? I have a tummy roll, cottage cheese on my thighs and bosoms that haven't perked in years."

Disrobing to reveal a body that isn't a young body dismays many of us older ladies, and should, even if it doesn't dismay many of the younger gals. Distressingly, I have noticed many younger women, by that I mean 30 to 40, who are already sporting fatty, cheesy badges of the good life as much or more as us more mature models.

I digress. That's their problem. In Chapter 2, "Fine-Tuning Your Appearance," I told you to lose weight if you are really overweight. Hopefully, you have remained plumpish, however. A plumpish mature woman is more juicy than a Le Cirque fencepost no matter how highly the fence posts are admired in the Big Apple.

So you've fine tuned and lost a bit, and you actually feel quite good about yourself, but you are sensible enough to know in your heart and mirror that you don't have a 16-year-old's body.

And you don't want to stand, lie or sit uncovered. There's your key, Toots. Don't ever, or practically ever, be totally uncovered. There is not a man alive who is not more fascinated by what he cannot see than what he can see.

Why do you think men of all ages flock to see

strippers? Not because the women are going to take it off, take it all off. He likes the thrill of peeping. The male sex is forever enthralled by what he cannot see of a woman's body.

Japanese men love necks, so Japanese women rarely reveal necks. Remember reading about the days when men went absolutely ape over an ankle? Don't give them too much of a good thing. Or don't give them too much of a bad thing if that's the case.

Give them sneak peeks. If you have great legs and a flabby middle, those cute little satin sleep shirts or see-through shortie nighties are for you. Do your thighs cause you sighs? No problem, dearie, just appear in a slinky long robe or nighties that falls to the floor, but leaves you deliciously décolleté on top. Sheer nylon robes or gowns that mask flaws and reveal only the delicious shimmer of skin are real turn-ons.

Waltz through the room in that, and he'll forget that the '49ers just blew the lead when there's only two minutes left to play. He'll forget the game and start making his own passes.

Don't love your feet? Seen too many miles, have they? Then get some nifty little slippers. Men like fluffy things.

There are so many styles of nightwear, lounging wear and underwear on the market, and in all price ranges, that finding just the right outfits to set off your particular attributes will be easy.

Just skip the bikini undies, will you, darling? Practically nobody over the age of 19 looks really good in a bikini. One afternoon on the beach at Waikiki can convince you of this. What can those women be thinking of? I watch them parading by, flab flopping in the soft breeze, and I wonder if they ever realize how absolutely unappealing they are. A man would have to be desperate or blind to turn to them in a moment of lust.

I'm preaching again. Let's just leave it at that. Be as wonderfully feminine as you really are and always remember how much fun it is to reveal just a flick of the forbidden than to rip off your clothes and destroy the mystique.

Don't forget to smell good. As I've lectured before, men love women who smell good. Don't knock their noses dead with a heavy musk, just a sweet lady scent to drive them out of their minds.

Looking good? Smelling good? Wonderful! Let's move on to the bed, or the floor, or the kitchen, or the front seat of his car.

How long has it been exactly since you smooched to desperation in the front sear of a car? That long? Good Lord, I hope you haven't forgotten how. Wanting to and not being able to is the greatest turn-on of all.

I remember what good old Marian told me one time. How she and her lover were on a vacation with their combined children. During an afternoon nap, Marian and Al started fooling around, the fooling feelings grew, and they became absolutely wild for each other.

But they knew they couldn't make any noise. Oh, God, she said. "It was absolutely wonderful. We could barely move, the bed squeaked, so we couldn't move, we couldn't utter a sound, those kids had ears like sonar. So we did it with barely a wiggle and barely a peep. It was so intense, it's a wonder we survived. We were limp as rags and needed a real nap when it was over."

What I'm getting to here is the fact that I hope you're not being one-way about sex. One-way meaning nights with the lights out, him getting on top of you, both bouncing around a little, and then whoof! It's over.

What do you mean that's the way you and Herbert always did it? Didn't I tell you about starting over?

There are three acts to the stage play of making love. The first act comes when the two players begin their mating dance. A hug, a kiss, a glimpse of stocking, you know. Something you have done or that he has done makes you want the closeness of togetherness. The realization hits that you're both ready and willing.

The second act: The actual act of making love.

And the third act: The curtain should ring down as you hold each other close, kissing and murmuring about how wonderful it has been.

Whoever said that action speaks louder than a thousand words has never consulted with a woman about sex.

Naturally, we love to be told we're pretty, we're touchable, we're lovable. How do you make him open his mouth and speak?

You tell him all those wonderful things. Unless he's a mute, he's going to be ashamed not to answer back. Tell him grunts don't count.

Where do you make love? Why, in the bed, of course! If that was you answering, you should be ashamed of yourself.

Practically anywhere outside of a shopping mall

concourse or your grandson's Little League game is permissible. Although the church picnic may not be the best place!

Joking aside, there's no law that says that act of love has to be committed on the marital bed.

Let me tell you about Ray and Ellie, both in their early sixties. To look at him, you'd think Ray was as strait-laced as any Grand PoohBah of the Mystic Herd of the Reindeer should be. Don't let looks fool you. Once Ellie had found the key to his heart, there were no holds barred, literally.

Like the time the couple was driving to her apartment after a dinner date. He suggested Ellie drive, pleading too much good bourbon and branch.

It was a warm evening but by the time they got to her place, the inside of the car was sizzling. Ray had driven Ellie to a frenzy with pats, strokes, kisses, caresses. Lord knows what else he did. He'd been a quarterback on the college team, and had never lost his quick hands.

When they got to her apartment, Ray and Ellie never made it past the tiny entrance hall. They simply made love on the carpet. It was a night neither of them will soon forget. Making it to the bed and in the bed simply never crossed their minds.

Some mid-chapter rules:

Rule One: Don't make any rules about where or how you're going to make love.

Rule Two: Relax.

Rule Three: Never ever forget your sense of humor.

Making love is not a do-or-die act. It should be love play, not love work.

Did you and Herbert ever experiment with positions? No? Well, perhaps you and Harry should. There's nothing nasty about you being on top. My friend Marian maintains it's the best possible position. But we all are different. It might help to invest in a book on sexual practices.

Not only will you learn new ways to put Leg A over Leg B which results in a lot of togetherness, you learn about things you never really thought about when you and Herbert were girls and boys together.

Like Oral Sex. O-Sex has been around for Lord knows how long. How do you think courtesans keep jaded monarchs alive and humming? Oriental paintings depict couples enjoying the act thousands of years ago.

Put that thing? In my mouth? I'd never do that, you're gagging right now, I can hear you.

Well, don't knock it until you've tried it, Xaviera Hollander once said.

Remember Xaviera, the Happy Hooker? She advocated practicing O-Sex on a peeled banana. Go ahead, try it. You might like it. HH Hollander claims it's a sure way to make him your slave forever. Never ever forget and bite. Instant deflation.

And as long as we're being grown ladies together, another suggestion. Many couples really enjoy watching an adult movie together. It can get the blood pounding. Skip hardcore American porn. With the smirking anti-heroes and silicon football breasts and bad acting in contrived sexual situations, it can be an awful turnoff.

Some good starters might be Koo Stark's *Emily* or the British version of *Lady Chatterly's Lover*. I don't know what it is about the British and porn, but they do porn better than we do. Maybe the photography of misty moors and elegant English country house weekends. The sex never looks gratituous, it looks torridly natural. Marian says that somehow they always put style into their sizzle.

Something all women know but rarely talk about: The biggest turn-on for a man is to know that they are turning on a woman. It is the greatest known aphrodisiac.

If you enjoy making love, enjoy the touching and the kisses, the intimate feeling of being really together, let him know it with sounds and sighs. Silent sex is hardly a stimulus.

Don't overlook the joy of a full body massage. Absolutely no one can refuse a massage. You don't have to be like the famous ladies of Bankok, the ones who offer body massages by massaging the other body with their own. Be traditional, use your hands. If you're never massaged muscles without using Ben-Gay, then you've a lovely surprise in store.

Get a book on the techniques. Buy some sweet-scented oil, warm it up; then lay him flat for a wonderful treatment. Will he like it? No man can resist it.

Now about those problem areas I spoke of in the beginning of this chapter. You and I both know that sexual failure for a man can happen at any age, and although most women are accustomed to failure to achieve orgasm on every occasion, men simply are not attuned to this. It's a do-or-die act for them.

So if there are problems, what do you do about them? You remove the pressure. Keep on with the hugs and the kisses, but stop short of any real sexual overtures.

Bob and Alice were having these problems, when Alice hit on a perfect solution. She'd read it somewhere. She suggested that when they went away on their little trips or stayed home with a good supper and a good tape on the VCR, they simply sleep together.

Really sleep, with no sex.

"I enjoy being in bed with you, I enjoy have you hold me and kiss me goodnight, but I don't really feel like sex tonight."

She doesn't really feel like sex tonight, but she wants me to hold her and kiss her while we're in the bed together? I know this thought ran wild in Bob's head.

But ever soliticious of her wants and desires, he agreed. After about four nights of this, he was wild with desire.

"I can't go on like this," he said, making a truly serious pass. "I have to have you. Right now!"

And he did. And they both loved it. And she smiled in her sleep at her cleverness.

"No, please, not tonight" works far better to cure impotence than powdered horn of the mystic white rhino.

There are some basic rules to remember when there are problems. Don't try to make love when you're both as full of food as beached whales after a herring feed. Never, never, ever (I can't shout this loud enough) try to make love when there's been one too many martinis. It simply won't work.

All right. The intimate wear has been upgraded; the body is sweet and feminine, the mind is in the right mood.

If you feel right about it and you make it right for him, then savor the luxuriousness of having the time and imagination to truly enjoy each other's bodies. There are no limits to the possibilities because a witty, compassionate and passionate woman is irresistible.

CHAPTER 9

GOING STEADY

Sharing Families and Friends May Not Be Easy

After a trial-and-error period of dating you probably had some experiences you couldn't wait to share with friends, your best friends, of course, because you don't recount your wild oats anymore than you want your date to recount his.

You've had some anguish, some fun and some crazies. Remember the guy whose toupee came off in the windstorm at the seventeenth hole? How about the guy who passed out on your couch? And the one who called you by his late wife's name during moments of passion?

Well, you've lived and you've learned. And you'll never forget these guys. Dating a variety before you settle down is a good idea. Certainly helps you separate the wheat from the chaff.

But now, ahhhh. You think you've discovered that special stalk of wheat with whom you want to really get serious.

Time out for a mini-quiz to see how things are progressing. The Q&As were prepared by Mike and Norma Slover, private practice counselors. Are you:

—Still in first blush, that period of time where everything he does looks wonderful, fresh and new? And so what if he has some warts, you'll learn to live with them or perhaps change them. Can you do either? Proceed with caution.

—Able to relax with him? Completely? My friend Marian says the best test of a relationship is if you can throw up in front of him and still face him the next day. Can you take it easy and let your warts and freckles show? Being able to show your weaknesses without fear of ridicule or humiliation is so very important to a relationship.

—Pretty well matched in sexual interests? Women's sexual interest seems to diminish when security needs are met, Norma Slover said. Men's drives are less likely to diminish. Is there a great amount of physical affection between you whether it leads to sex or not?

—A toucher and he never learned how? It may not seem important now, but if you're thinking of a committment, it could be very lonely to live without affection outside the bedroom.

—Trying to change him? Don't make any long-range plans with this guy if you have a grocery list of changes you plan to make after you've got the ring on your finger. It's not fair to him and you'll be miserable.

– Able to make concessions about activities?

– Able to resolve conflicts? How do you each deal with anger? Are you both screamers? Get it out in the open; then make up? Is one a screamer, the other a sulker? Is making up hard to do?

– Nurturing and being nurtured? Is there enough talking and taking care of going on in this twosome? Getting enough of those precious little "There, there, baby's" that every woman needs from time time. If there are times you feel like you're a stranger in a strange world, get going. This isn't healthy.

– Able to compromise on important decisions? You're more of a grown-up woman than you were when you began dating, but you've still got to be able to make compromises about children and friends of your be-loved. More about the children's hour and friends later.

– Well matched in religious and political beliefs? Or relatively compatible? A different view of religion can often sour a relatively good relationship. If one is a believer, the other an atheist, it will be difficult unless you are adult enough not to force your opinions on each other.

– Agreed on social values? Work ethics? Sexual values?

– Able to put your partner's needs above your own? Not constantly, but are you able to evaluate the situation at hand and, if needed, sublimate your wishes?

– Able to meet half way if the issue is a serious one?

You're not going to be graded on this quiz. Only

you know what you answered. Above all, I hope you
were honest with yourself. How did the relationship
fare?

Very well? Good! If you were able to answer yes to
all save the first question, then let's talk about what is
the single most cause of breakup in an adult union.

Not money, not sex. It's children, said Father Willis
Steinberg of St. Paul's Episcopal Church in Salem, Oregon.

His opinion is widely shared by those who counsel
adults on their second unions.

"But they're all grown up with families of their
own," you in all your innocence protest. "Why won't
they be happy to see their father loved and taken care
of?"

Why indeed? Will we ever know what goes on in the
heads of children about parental dating and marriage?

Even the most sane of children can suffer from
pangs when they see a happy mother curling her hair
and preparing for a date with a man other than their own
father. Even the most balanced of young adults turn
snarly when a woman comes into their father's lives and
begins acting like a mother.

If there's been a divorce, the kids, even the most
mature, can say:

"Well if you'd tried harder, you'd still be with Dad."

Does this hurt? Well, of course it hurts. If you have
been a wise mother, you didn't share all your former
husband's foibles with your kids? What good would it
have done you to weep and wail about the perfume you
smelled when he sneaked into bed after those "late
office work" nights?

Remember the night he told you frankly and cruelly, "You're old and ugly and I don't want to live with you anymore. Donna and I are far more compatible than you and I ever were."

But you didn't tell the children. What would that have accomplished? A wise and compassionate mother never confides pain or problems to a child unless that child is able to do something about the situation.

You may have bitter memories of what your husband was like as a husband, but if he wasn't physically and verbally abusive in front of the children or a high-profile alcoholic, they won't know what you suffered. And they never will because you love them and don't want to spoil their memories of Daddy.

So when they make snide comments about your dating and your new love, it will cut to the quick. Kids are perfect wizards at loading a parent up with guilt about spending so much time with Howard that you no longer have time to be a mother.

Your head is telling you that you've been a mother for the better part of your life and can you please slow down and relax now? Of course not, you never stop being a mother.

What's to do?

You sit down with them, tell them that you love them above all others, but it is time to get on with your life. You assure them that you will never abandon them even though they are grown and are making more money than you ever earned in your life. Tell them they are still your beloved kiddos and you're still a family.

But strive to make them realize that you are a grown woman who needs the love and companionship necessary for any woman's complete happiness.

If they're adults, they'll simmer down and eventually accept the situation IF you keep your promises to them.

If they are brats and carry on a blood feud, then look them in the eye and say, "I love you very much and I'm sorry you feel this way, but you have a big problem I'm not able to help you with. Have you considered counseling?"

Wow! As a mother can you utter those words? It may be the hardest thing you've ever had to do, but unless you want to become a slave to your spoiled adult children, you're going to have to open your mouth and speak up for your own rights. Stick to your guns and carry through with your own life.

Only you allow you to become a victim. Do not seek help from your sweetheart. Dealing with your children is not something your new love will be able to help you with, nor should you expect him to.

All right. You have your side of the family pretty well taken care of, now what about his side?

This is not always easy. Your kids may feel left out, but they do, at heart, love you. His kids don't have this to fall back on. All they see is a woman who is out to take their rightful place in their father's heart and they're going to make it as difficult as possible.

The ways stepchildren can harass a stepmother are as varied as are prospective stepchildren and prospective stepmothers. The tales I have heard can turn your hair white right through your L'Oreal wash-gray-away-rinse.

You want a few tales of terror? Will they make you feel better? Well, you're not going to get any except the stories I've heard range from nasty words, "mis placed letters and phone calls," sly pranks, threatened suicide, invasion of privacy and actual physical violence. Just believe that whatever you're going through has been gone through before and will be gone through by other women in other relationships.

I won't divulge confidences here, but following are some tips from stepmothers who have been there and survived.

Forewarned is forearmed. Here goes:

−If you celebrate Christmases together, make sure that each side has a stated number of gifts to open. Faces can freeze if one side has three times the number of gifts or more expensive trinkets. Make sure both sides get treated fairly.

−Leave some holidays open so father and his children can celebrate alone together if they so choose.

−Be understanding about weddings. If there's a biggie on his side and you are not formally engaged, simply suggest that you don't attend if the kids' mother will be present. When you're married, that's another story.

−If there are actually harsh words, do as I instructed you to do with your own children. Tell them you're sorry they feel that way and shut up. Don't apologize. Don't explain. They're adults and should be mature enough to know their father is his own person.

−If father doesn't have enough courage to tell them to back off and treat you with respect, then the problem is indeed grave and I would extricate myself from the relationship. If he won't stand up for you when you're good friends, he'd be less likely to after marriage and life would become a living hell for the both of you. Remove yourself and tell yourself it's his loss. It is.

If the children like and accept you, count yourself twice blessed and try to be a good friend to them. Don't try to be their mother. You are not now and you never will be. But good friends they'll appreciate.

Now about the grandchildren. Introduce your loved ones to him and arrange for him to introduce his to you. If you're lucky as I was, it will be easy to love his grandkids, but in some cases, in today's peer pressure world, it will not be a fun break. But make an effort and never stop trying. Sometimes it works well to get the grandkids together without grown-ups. You may never manage to get the first generation to be good friends, but you may triumph with the second.

Speaking of good friends. Let's talk about them. Love him, hate his friends? It happens all the time.

These problem friends generally fall into three main categories:

1. Those who knew your sweetheart when he was married to the first wife. They're still living in the good old days and conversations generally begin, "Remember when . . .?"

2. Parasites. They had your sweetheart to themselves for lo these many years and they're not about to share their free ride with a woman who will see them for what they really are—after his time and his money. Their demands are outrageous to all but your sweetheart who is a really good guy and wants to help his old buddies.

3. Goodtime buddies. Generally, there is not a wife

involved in this male-male friendship. Your sweet-hearthas always played golf three times a week, bowled two nights and been available for buddy/buddy beer binges. This friend has lost his pal and he will resent you as an interloper.

Your methods of dealing with these problems differ with the problems.

Be patient with the friends who knew him when, but don't feel that you have to sit and listen forever to the memories of Good Old Days. Can you be outspoken enough to say, "Hey, I wasn't there then. Let's go out and make some memories of our own." Or change the conversation to something the four of you have planned for the future. Be nice to these folks. They probably don't even realize that you are hurt or offended. They are just trying to hold on to your sweetheart's company. Be kind. Be patient. Smile through your gritted teeth as you listen once more to how well the ex-wife entertained or the vacations together with the late wife.

Parasites are another breed to deal with and very difficult. Lynn married Greg, a successful doctor. A good surgeon, a good doctor, but a bad businessman, Greg had become the prey of a catalog of parasites from those who "had such a good deal, you've got to get in on it," to the "I have this little pain" variety.

As a result, Greg and Lynn's home was a mad scene of parasites coming with hands out and midnight phone calls. If they didn't want money, they wanted free medical advice. The marriage was a morass of "Gimmes" from people who ignored Lynn to get to Greg.

One guy arrived with his old wife and a new girl-friend. When the visit ended, he exited with the new girlfriend and left the old wife behind for Greg to "find a job and help her get started."

Incredible? It's true. Because Greg's ego was so entwined with the parasites to whom he felt he was the Almighty Father, the marriage never had a chance. Lynn made the sad discovery that he, like many doctors, enjoyed being the Almighty Father.

He's still handing out time and money. Lynn has gone onto a new career and a new life. A pity because these two loved each other.

If your sweetheart is surrounded with parasites, work very hard to get him interested in healthy non-demanding friendships and activities. But good luck, it will not be easy.

The buddy/buddy who wants all your man's time is a bit easier to deal with than parasites. Just give your man so much love and fun attention that he doesn't mind saying "No" when Bud calls with offers for beer binges, bowling, hunting, fishing or whatever.

If you detect a pattern to the requests, be clever enough to have something better planned for the evenings Bud requests. But be subtle, please. Men are very quick to know when they are being manipulated.

If you and your darling have managed to calm the children's fears that they will be neglected, kept the desirable old friends while going out to make new friends on your own and are dedicated to making each other feel loved, happy, comfortable and lusted after, then you have a wonderful chance of making your relationship a lasting one.

CHAPTER 10

THE BAD GUYS

They Don't Always Wear Black Hats

Unless you meet a winner on the first date, sometime you're going to meet the type of fellow our grandfathers labelled rotters, cads, and lechers. If you were around during World War II, you knew them as "wolves." Their presence was always signaled by a long, low whistle that was music to a girl's ears.

Appreciation is music to any woman's ears, but today's wolves aren't in the game for a peek and a whistle. They are far more dangerous because of the mind games they play. Their prey is women who have been alone too long and are eager, sometimes desperate, for affection. A man whose primary goal is seduction for self-gratification can be extremely hazardous to a woman whose defenses are down. Unfortunately,

149

some of these fellows come wrapped in attractive packages.

When we were girls, we had our fathers right there to reinforce the morals and values so carefully taught us by our mothers. Being young and frisky, we didn't really appreciate the zealousness with which our fathers guarded us—their most precious treasures. We were doubly protected by our youthful and natural instincts to beware of the unknown, and the unknown then was sex.

In mid-life, we know that sex is fun, so our defenses may crumble even though we are aware that danger may lurk behind that easy grin and a knowing glance. But there is no protective parent to save us now. We have only ourselves.

The predators come in all shapes and all sizes. Some are easy to spot because these louts haven't bothered to update their techniques since high school. These teenage studs grown older are still practicing the same busy fingers routine they tried behind the bleachers so many years ago. Smartie that you are now, you can send those guys packing with a few choice words. It's the subtle predators who are more deadly. If you enjoy taking risks and are itching for the spice of danger, you may give these guys a twirl or two, but don't give them your heart. These guys are simply in the game to score.

Some bed veterans make no secret of their conquests and wear their women like battle ribbons. Others are too clever by half to make their sexual prowess known.

A new danger in our society is the nice guys we dated in high school and college. They obeyed the rules then, but today's new rules and new games have overwhelmed them. They may have been loving and non-cheating husbands for years, but contemporary society's sexual permissiveness has made them as greedily horny as a bull gone wild in a harem of heifers. These men are caught in the midst of mid-life crisis and they do things they normally wouldn't think of doing. However, this is no excuse for their ratty behavior.

May I pause here for a medical lecture? Don't turn away. This is important. Despite our age, we are not immune to sexually transmitted diseases and AIDS. So it is vital to learn as much as possible about the sexual provenance of the guy you're interested in.

Be realistic. You're not going to discover an untapped 55-year-old virgin. (Who wants one?) The man you're going to find has known women, and every man is entitled to his sexual privacy—but you do have a right to know where he's been.

Older heterosexual males can be pretty naïve about sexual encounters. Perhaps, because they haven't had to think about social diseases since their GI training film days. These darlings generally read things like *Golf Digest* and *Field and Stream*. The self-help books and magazine articles women devour by the dozens aren't on men's best-seller lists.

One well-meaning male friend sent a new widower a paid-in-advance young prostitute. The widower was lonely and a little bit drunk when the frisky lovely, barely out of her teens, arrived to console him. They had a perfectly marvelous time—he was sure she had as good a time as he did. But within days, he turned up with an embarrassing case of gonorrhea. Having to explain it to a physician made him thrice shy of encounters for months after.

There is no way of making absolutely sure a man is
sexually healthy because even the nicest guys can take a
tumble with a sleep-around who only God remembers
where she's been. I'll warn you right now that many
older men think wearing condoms is just not macho. In
days gone by, the only things they had to worry about
was gonorrhea, which could be cured, or the woman's
pregnancy, which was her responsibility, wasn't it?

If you have any doubts about where your guy's
been, don't be stupid and turn modest. It's tough to
think of whipping a condom out of your ladylike alliga-
tor bag, but forget dignity. The action may save your
life.

Now, let's get going on how to spot the potentially
dangerous guy before he's zeroed in and captured your
heart and soul. How can you avoid possible physical
and emotional damage?

First I'll give you some "Watch out for these guys"
case histories; then we'll go into detective work.

Macho Mannie: That's not his real name because
his real name doesn't matter. We've all known him.
Dangerously attractive in our high school years, our
fathers turned pale if a Mannie turned up on the family
doorstep. Whenever there was a scrape, a tussle, some
action, Macho Mannie was in the forefront, muscles
rippling against his white T-shirt, tousled forelock
hanging over his eye, and a ciggie dangling from his lip.

As attractive, but far less lovable, as Fonzie of
"Happy Days" fame, Mannie swaggered across our
high school hearts. But as the good little A-group girls
we were, we never dated him. So he played fast and

loose with the B and C group girls who succumbed to his charms.

Mannie always had a superior built-in hostility against women—was there a detested mother lurking around in his past? His idea of living it up was putting women down. He chalked up conquests on his private totem. Unfortunately, Mannie always found plenty of victims ready and willing for his brand of lovemaking.

Forty years later, the Macho Mannies of the world still get more than their rightful share of loving. Sure, that wavy pompadour we remember has thinned, and all that beer they chugged rolls around their middles, but the Mannies still have that cock-of-the walk swagger, that knowledgeable glint in their eye, and that hand on the door lest things get too heavy.

In one other detestable way, Macho hasn't changed with time. He'll still tell all who will listen about his conquests.

The Mannies of the world can be found most often in singles clubs. By joining a singles club, a woman announces that she is lonely, and in Mannie's pea-sized brain, this declaration is synonymous with sexually deprived.

One Mannie of my acquaintance invited me to a singles club dance, but assured me that he had no designs on me.

"I can always get taken care," he bragged.

That's Mannie's way of saying he can be sexually serviced whenever he so chooses. I don't think the term "make love" has ever crossed his lips. In his world, women aren't there to make love to; they are there to cater to his sexual needs.

And most definitely, that is not what I want for you. You deserve far more.

Jump-off Jack: Watch out for this one. He's a hit and run artist with an almost perfect record of seduction. He is uncanny in sensing exactly what a woman wants and needs—or thinks she needs. Of all the bed veteran categories, Jack is the most dangerous because he is truly a likable and extremely intelligent guy, an ingratiating mixture of sophistication and "aw shucks!"

Because he's been perfecting this technique since long before his marriage was over, Jack has a subtle but dynamite approach. It begins with eye contact across a crowded room. The look is not lecherous. It is slow and meaningful, a sort of "I've been waiting for you. Where have you been?"

Jack rarely has to move toward a woman; he charms as surely as a cobra. And women react just as predictably as a moth checking out a flame. If for some reason a woman does not catch the eye contact from afar, he appears at her elbow to throw her an optic whammy at close range.

His approach is pseudo-philosophical. He throws out a remark about a burning issue to plumb her depths of social understanding. It's a thinly-veiled challenge. How about a platonic sexual relationship? Would this type relationship be possible between two consulting adults?

Jump-off is nearly impossible to resist. There's a sparkle in his eye that says "You and me kid, we're different. They're them, and we're us." Before you know it, you, the savviest of intellectual ladies, will find

yourself discussing the dire state of the nation today—
and in bed after you've made love.

Make any attempt to get serious, and Jack lives up
to his nickname of Jump-off. He can jump off a relationship fast as a snake can slither across hot tarmac.

He is, he will tell you with much sighing and much
deep eye contact, he is incapable of a lasting relationship. Something, he bemoans, is wrong with him.
Something is left out. He's not whole.

Intelligent women, who should know better, will
continue to pursue Jump-off because they think that
they alone can cure this terrible curse. They alone can
create wholeness where there is a void. They believe
that if he receives all their devotion, he will be healed.
Silly girls. He's one step ahead of them all the way.

And then she is left—alone again—and somehow,
she anguishes, it was her fault, her lack. It is awhile
before you begin to wonder if his poor wife really died
of a brain tumor or was it a broken heart?

I'm not saying avoid Jump-offs altogether because a
whirl with Jump-off can broaden your mind and sexual
expertise. After all, he is masterful at making love.

The instant you detect that you are just another
chapter in his autobiography, jump off first. And forever after, you can be the one to savor the pleasure of
watching his face as you tell him, "I'm sorry, darling.
We came close, didn't we?" Jump-off Jacks loathe being
dumped first. It's an unpleasant shock to their very big
egos and certainly not in their Big Picture.

Jump-off's grazing grounds can be anywhere. This
man is never tacky or obvious, but he is none the less
lethal for all his class action. He's at his best in darkened

bars or private parties. He's been known to seduce in the supermarket aisles, political parties, government meetings and church suppers.

Peter Rabbit: He's another danger to avoid, because this bunny bites. When Peter looks at you and tells you that he had to learn to touch, your heart goes out to this lovable creature. He's worked so hard so many years. He's never had any fun, poor thing. And now, at last, he is able to have fun.

Life will be fun with Peter. He'll take you places you've never been and always wanted to go. He'll send ego-boosting bouquets to your office. Dinners are always in all the best places. (Should you worry when the maitre d' calls him by name and asks if he wants his regular table? Yes!) He'll offer you romantic cruises on a sternwheeler. "Show me your world, and I'll show you mine" is Peter's line, and it's easy to fall for. Fun is something that has been in short supply for you lately.

You're bedazzled by Peter's hip hopping. This life, too, can be yours, if only you can slow Peter down long enough to cuddle him, show him what life with a really good woman can do for him. He needs your chicken and dumplings and the apple pie his uncaring mother never made him.

He didn't have it good in his first marriage. She didn't understand him, didn't realize that he was working for a purpose. She should have accepted all those solo dinners with three kids under five. He was struggling for success and, now he's entitled to his fun.

And you're going right with him.

Sure you are, baby, right into the looney bin. It takes a while to figure out that whatever floats Peter's boat is not what floats yours. What floats it is that he's going to jump every body he possibly can before the final whistle. He can't help it. He was deprived of childhood and boyhood, and he's making every moment left count.

The clever appliquéd pillow (probably made by some cute little bunny) in the back seat of his car should have been your first clue that Peter Rabbit hops from bed to bed to bed. He'll always be your friend, but he won't always be your lover. He's too busy working the garden patch to see how many carrots are left undug.

Peter's preferred patches are business mixers, community affairs and civic functions. He's light years ahead of Macho Mannie when it comes to class and poor old Macho doesn't have half the action that Peter has without even trying. Peter, bless him, is a wonderful and lovable fellow who means no harm to anyone, is always in the right place at the right time. Even after Peter's hopped off, he still manages to make you feel special when he nibbles on your ear at a dinner dance. No matter if he's got a dolly half his age on his arm, he'll always be a friend. Just don't ask for anything more.

Fast-Lane Frankie: Now, he's really one to watch. He's a wheeler and he's a dealer as he moves down the highway of life. Tall, dark and handsome, ever so slightly sleazy, Frankie is on the fringes of a world I hope you never enter. He's a money man, always playing the odds. Frankie's got an about-to-be-ex wife, but she's so much in the picture that one's never sure if she knows she's about to be ex. But Frankie has told you the divorce has been filed; it's simply a matter of time.

You met him at a political fund-raiser, and you

were immediately attracted by his take-charge arro-
gance, his London-tailored suit, the Piaget on his wrist,
and the diamond on his pinkie. He was surrounded by
a group of people you had never met, but somehow he
began looking at you. The next thing you knew he was
beside you, holding out a glass of champagne.

Frankie is everything exciting you didn't have the
first time around. He lives in a world of "comps." To
Frankie, it's not worth having unless it's been
"comped" by the big money boys. Pay for the pro
basketball game? Not on your life, Toots. Frankie's tick-
ets have been "comped" by the management, and
they're front row center. Zip off to Vegas? To Atlantic
City? The private plane will be here at 5 P.M., babe, so
be ready. Take in a '49er game? Pack your bag; we're
leaving. Don't worry, darling. Frankie will take care of
it.

And he needs you. He needs you to give credibility
to his social life. With a class act like you on his arm, his
social cachet is assured. Together you're a team, and
you begin to be invited as such.

When you're at home alone together, he cuddles
up in your arms like a tired little boy. His head hurts.
You're there to rub it. Tension in his neck? Certainly
Mama will ease out all those little spasms.

If he doesn't have a lot of time for you, you're sure
to understand. In the world of big finance—and Frankie
always makes his financial world sound big—you know
you're out of your league, and you leave business up to
him. He's got to work hard to afford all the toys he
surrounds himself with. But what is it exactly that he
does? Sometimes it's not really apparent.

If you are still working, you work extra hard during

the days you don't see him to make up for the times you do, because when Frankie wants you, he wants all your time. Your job isn't really that important, is it?

There's a secret side to Frankie's life that you keep pushing to the back of your brain because this man really needs you. There was the night he snuggled up and suggested you smoke marijuana together because it had "been a bitch of a day." But you began to worry about Frankie. Something's not quite right. Then there was the night you arrived at his apartment and found the $100 bills curled up on the coffee table, and the good old U.S. green was decorated with specks of red. "What's this, darling?" you asked. "Bleed all over your money?"

He shrugged and said, "Big money boys from Vegas were down. They needed some party favors. Can't use straws with those boys."

And then you knew for sure. Frankie's mood swings weren't from real moods. His moods were self-induced moods; self-induced by some uppers he'd told you were vitamins; the downers he took every night and swore they were aspirins. They were funny-colored aspirins, but you weren't raised in a world of drugs, so you really didn't know.

But you know now. And you know why Frankie isn't able to get it up too much any more. Well, sure, he's really 60 years old, you reason, but in your heart you know the real reason. Frankie is living a hard life on the edge, a life filled with half-dealt deals and drugs that heighten the pleasures or numb the pain.

This little scenario may have sounded like a half-finished chapter of a Grade B novel, but these men do exist, even in small towns. I know wonderful women

who have succumbed to the lure of the unknown. If a
Fast-Lane Frankie should speed into your life, just pull
over and let him pass you by. He's more trouble than
you'd ever want to know about.

P.S: Don't ever let Fast-Lane talk you into a business deal and don't ever lend him any money.

Frankie's fields are the hot spots; the "in" restaurants, the newest lounges; private clubs, and sporting
events. You may run across him at $100-a-plate fund-
raisers. No wine and cheese benefits for our Frank. He
looks high class, but that's just his little lie.

Macho Mannie, Jump-off Jack, Peter Rabbit, and
Fast-Lane Frankie are four of the most serious bed hop-
pers you may encounter in your reentry. I hope they're
a bit easier to spot with these profiles.

There are other blights like the heavy-duty per-
suader. "Why don't you sleep with me? It isn't good for
me to let you just take me so far."

And then he goes into the routine of it being bad
for his health. Would you believe, darling, that there
are some guys out there still using the old "my testicles
will rot if you don't let me" routine. The same whines
you heard in the 1938 convertible are being trotted out
today. Pay less attention to the "poor me" routine than
you did then when all that was keeping you virginal
was the knowledge that good girls didn't do things like
that.

Be careful of bullies, too. "I take you out, I buy you
a good dinner, and what happens? I want a little love,
and you turn me off. You don't really like me, or you
would."

Some guys don't fall into any particular category,
but they can be dangerous to you simply because you

are you. Women who are unable to display dominant tendencies generally look for men who are over-endowed in the aggressive department. They seem to be drawn to the men who project the qualities they lack.

If you find yourself falling for a bossy guy, take some time out to figure out why this type turns you on. You probably turn him on because he has a sadistic streak that covers a wimp-weak underbelly.

Most women do like a bit of the take-charge in a guy. But if he goes overboard at telling you what to do and when to do it, run a mile in the opposite direction. Bossy boyfriends make perfectly awful domineering husbands.

By the same token, a man who is sensitive and caring to you but seems unable to make it in the marketplace is often a man who will seek out the strong and dominant woman. Sometimes this mix is a match—as long as it is livable to you.

How best to spot and avoid the men who have the ability to damage your heart and soul?

– ASK. You're rarely going to meet a man that no one knows. Granted, Maggie met a plumber in the fish market. A hunch told her that he was an okay guy, so she went out with him. On the third date, he suggested doubling with friends—his. While not as mentally stimulating as her plumber, the friends were nice honest folks, so she queried the wife, and got the right answers.

Naturally, you're not going to ask the guy's ex-wife what sort of husband material he is, but on the other hand, don't discount any rumors and seek a source if possible. It's not sneaky; it's just good sense.

– STOP. Or at least go slowly when it comes to

offering your finest asset—yourself. Women suffer devastating emotional pain when they discover it was only
basic lust that motivated a man to whisper sweet noth-
ings and future everythings.

Jenny thought Al would never make the move.
After months of dating, he still hadn't popped the
"Why don't we . . . ?" What he did do was arrive at her
door one evening, screwdriver in hand, and offer to put
together some bookcases she'd purchased.

After two hours of blood (on his thumb), sweat (on
his brow), and near tears (in an attempt to help, she'd
dropped a shelf on his head), the bookcases were finished, and she knew this man was for keeps.

"I think the moment that I dropped the shelf on his
head, and he didn't yell at me, was the moment I began
to love him," she recalls. "Right then I felt that we were
a couple."

When Al finally got around to suggesting a weekend in Lake Tahoe, the two were already so mentally
close in shared memories, the physical relationship was
warm, natural and comfortable. And she discovered
that Al was as handy in bed as he was with a screwdriver.

Don't be snowed by glittering generalities; wait for
the slow but sure specifics. A woman who is too quickly
swept off her feet is too often swept into the gutter by a
callous lover.

– LOOK. Look at how he treats his friends, how he
treats you when you are with his friends, and how he
treats your children, even the ornery ones. Look at how
he treats waiters and clerks. Being abusive to a person
in a subservient position can be the true measure of a
person.

When Maggie dated Loyd the plumber, she noticed that he was caring, affectionate, and sensitive to the fact that she did not know these people. He made every effort to draw her into the conversation and never left her twisting slowly in the wind with "Remember when . . . " exchanges with his chums.

– LISTEN. Listen to what he says, and listen to the kind of jokes he tells. If they are jokes where men are always doing it to women, you know that is his sexual mentality. If you detest a "Women are here to do it to" attitude, run for your life. Not only will he be lousy in bed, he'll be lousy for your head, and you don't need head problems.

My chum, Gracie, the one with the popular restaurant and lounge on the Oregon coast, has heard all the lines there are. "And the worst is a guy who blows his balloon so full of hot air I'm afraid my roof will fly away," she said.

"If a man is so full of himself he can't talk about anything else, turn off your mind, and head for the powder room. He's not a keeper."

Of course you want a physical relationship sooner or later, but certainly not at the expense of your self-respect, your soul, and your health.

What we want for you is a man who is strong but objective in his outlook on life, a man who is emotionally balanced and can express himself. You want a man who will encourage you to be all that you can be.

CHAPTER 11

YOU'RE IN LOVE

But He's a Boy and You're a Woman

Keeping an upbeat attitude is the surest way I know of to cast aside doubt and head out into the mainstream. But—there's that awful word—I'm going to be a bit negative in this chapter. Bear with me, I'm only doing it to protect you.

Here's the scenario: You've found love's dream, and you've never had so much fun. There's only one problem, and it keeps coming back to haunt like the blood on the castle floor that can't be washed away.

You're in love, but your love is younger than you. How much younger? Well, if you were a precocious teenager and had ventured out into a sexual world, you

165

could conceivably (pun intended) have mothered this man. Ouch!

Let's hear from a few grandmothers on this situation, which is extremely common in today's society.

Kate: She is a 46-year-old divorcée with a good job in state government. Her only child, a daughter, lives about two hundred and fifty miles away and visits once or twice a year. Kate is active in a great many groups. She met Cam at a political fund-raiser.

"It was a fascinating experience that had me tingling for days afterward," Kate said. "I stepped outside to smoke and was just standing, listening to the candidate's speech. From out of nowhere this guy appeared to light my cigarette. He lit it, then said, "He (the candidate) is completely skirting the real issue in favor of a simplistic gut issue that will bring in the votes."

"Amazingly, this was exactly what was going through my head at the time," she said. "I couldn't believe this boy had so accurately picked up my thoughts. This guy was a real hunk with broad shoulders, narrow waist, streaked blond hair. He could have passed as a beach boy, but his young fogey wire-rim glasses and suit made him look worldly and wise.

"We kept on talking about politics. Then he asked if I wanted to have a glass of wine at LeBistro, a little place nearby. My mind was telling me, 'Kate, this is a boy,' but every womanly cell in me was zinging that this was someone I'd like to know better.

"I'm not going to pull any punches. I took Cam home with me that night, and we lived together for six months."

He was, Kate discovered, 32 to her 44, and employed in a low-level state job although he had plans for the future. Cam had earned his degree in political science and a master's in business, while Kate had quit college in order to get married and have babies.

"His education, and my lack of it made him the superior being, in my mind. We were perfectly matched physically," Kate said. "I think 44 is the sexiest age a woman can be, and at 32 he was full steam ahead. I could swear we didn't get out of bed for a week, and when we did we never lacked for things to talk about. It was a slice of heaven that I, at 44, never expected to have."

So what happened?

Well, Kate's daughter came to visit with the two grandchildren. Did Cam resent the intrusion? Far from it. He and daughter Nell hit it off beautifully, although Nell was a little concerned that her mother might eventually be hurt in this relationship. There didn't seem to be any problem. Cam adored the children, and Kate was delighted with the ease of the situation.

About three weeks after Nell and the children left, troubles appeared in Paradise. Cam began having mood swings. There were days he loved Kate to physical distraction; other days he would barely speak to her.

Finally, Kate got up enough courage to ask him what was wrong.

"I said, 'Cam, we've been a lot to each other, and the way you're behaving is very hurtful. Please tell me what is wrong.'"

Amazingly, Cam began to cry.

"I'd never seen a man cry before," Kate said, "and it was very unnerving. He came over and put his arms around me and said, 'I'm so sorry.'"

And then it all came out. Cam had become interested in a young woman at the Capitol. The crux of the matter soon surfaced.

"Cam said that his office romance was just a flirty-flirty thing until Nell and the children came to visit. He said he loved my grandchildren. Then it began to rankle that he didn't have any children of his own. He cried harder when he said said he didn't want to hurt me, but Kimberly, that was the girl's name, could give him his own children."

Brutal words those. "Kimberly could give him his own children."

"I may sound overly dramatic, but that sentence was like a knife in my heart. There it was. The truth. Cam held me and kissed me and told me how much he loved me, but he had to get on with his life. He was telling me that I was just a pleasant interlude, and getting on with his life did not include me," Kate said.

Kate said that at first, even the sound of the name Kimberly "made me furious. It was such a young and trendy name. I could just see this Kimberly. Long blond hair, long skinny body, and not a wrinkle on her face. I hated the girl, and I hadn't even met her."

Eventually, Kate did meet Kimberly, who wasn't a blonde nymphet, simply a nice young woman who worked in the stenography pool.

What hurt the most was the day Cam brought Kimberly to meet her.

"I felt like Cam's mother looking over the prospective bride," Kate said. "I never felt any older in my entire life, which, incidentally, I felt was over at that moment. I remember standing there thinking, 'This is the moment I grew old.' I will never forget it."

Cam came to visit Kate one last time. He kissed her,

thanked her for being wise and wonderful, and assured her that it wasn't that he didn't love her; the paths of their lives had to take different directions.

Kate hasn't forgotten the moment she felt old, but she is a strong enough woman to have wished Cam and Kimberly well and moved past the attachment. She is now dating a state administrator who is in his fifties. "With him, I don't think about age at all, and we are very happy doing the things we do," she said.

Lest you be distressed about Kate's activities, they are most definitely not "old" things. She and the administrator have joined a winter sports club, and now cross country ski during the winter. In the summer, they play golf, and when it's raining, they make a lot of love.

"It isn't burning hot young love, but it's good love," Kate said.

Alison: Fresh from a bitter divorce and the death of her father, Alison took a tour of Italy. Florence's grandeur, Venice's fading splendor, and Rome's *joie de vivre* were doing their part to fight the 52-year-old woman's gloomy outlook on life. In Rome, Alison and her tour friends went out to dinner one evening.

"Two other single women and I were in a Roman trattoria ordering dinner," she said. "The waiter helping us translate the menu was so unbelievably handsome we kept exclaiming over him. He was sort of a cross between an Italian Mel Gibson and a Spanish Tom Cruise. His laughter at our atrocious Italian accents was so infectious that my own gloom began to lift.

"The other two women were quite a bit younger than I was, so when they asked the waiter where the town's liveliest disco was, I paid no attention. The last thing I wanted to do was be surrounded by gorgeous young bodies. My husband, Nate, had left me for a younger woman, and I didn't want to suffer by comparison.

"The next thing I knew, my friends were making a date with the waiter, whose name was Vito, to meet him and two of his friends at La Trendia, a disco near the Spanish Steps.

I said, 'Hey, guys, leave me out of this. I'm not a disco dolly. I'm too old.'

"Well, Vito knew enough English to understand that, and he began protesting. Finally, he took my hand, and said, 'For me, you come.'

"My friends urged, and I finally capitulated, thinking, 'Well, why not?' To make it short, I had the most wonderful time of my life. I thoroughly agreed with the wit who bemoaned the fact that youth is wasted on the very young.

"Yes, Vito was my escort, my partner for that evening, and he made me feel young. We did everything that you dream about doing in Rome. He made me feel about 18 years old. We threw coins into the Trevi Fountain. He reached in and drew out a coin for me so I could 'remember the evening.' We ended up sitting on the Spanish Steps at 3 A.M. Those Italians never want to go to bed. Vito teased me, telling me that 'Romans only go to bed in the early afternoon, and not to sleep,' He was a handsome, sensuous young man, well tuned in to the Roman world around him.

"Yes, I did sleep with him during the five days we spent in Rome. It was the most romantic time I'd ever had, a time a woman would dream about, but there were moments that I was terrified. I can't really explain it. Young Italian men are different from men over here.

"Their culture is not our culture. His brand of love-making took so many forms. One moment I was his cuddly baby; the next time, he would be loud and braggadocio and take me as if I was an object, not a person. His temper tantrums ranged from lovable child to naughty brat to a cynical man I didn't really want to be around. When the time came to part, it was difficult, but in a way I felt like I was free again. He was very possessive with me, obsessively so for such a short acquaintance.

"All I can say about older women and younger men is that my dalliance in Rome with Vito was something I'll never forget, but I wouldn't want to repeat it. Maybe it was a clash of cultures, or maybe it was the difference in ages. I believe age is relevant, but I'm just past living for the moment. Vito wants to come over here to visit, but I'm not too anxious to have him here. We are too different. He isn't anyone I could ever count on, and I need to protect myself."

Janine: "I began seeing a younger man last August. He was fun, he was caring, and I enjoyed our time together. I guess it ended when I realized that I repre-sented security to him. It was funny, sort of a older man/younger woman relationship, but in reverse. He looked to me to provide him with security.

"Jake was proud of the fact that I owned a nice house, drove a nice car and had a membership in a golf club. He moved in on my life, and it took me awhile to figure out that it was my life-style he was intrigued with and not me especially. Did it hurt? Hell, yes, but I had to break it off."

Nancy: "My love affair with a younger man was short and sweet while it lasted. It lasted until Billy dropped over one night; when my daughters were home from college. The next thing I knew they had put on the CDs and were teaching Billy the newest dances. I was in the kitchen fixing supper, and they were in the family room dancing their little hearts out. When I called them for supper, I realized that I was calling my kids in to supper, and one of the kids was the man I was sleeping with. Put it in that perspective and you can lose interest real fast. I told Billy the next day that it was over, and he came all unglued. He thought I was jealous of him dancing with the girls and promised never to do anything like that. I pride myself on the fact that I told him he should be doing things like that. He was the right age. We parted friends."

The stories of Kate, Alison, Janine and Nancy may sound dramatic, but such is often the case with May-December romances when December's on the woman's side.

Vickie's story is less dramatic but equally poignant. Vickie is a more-than-plump person with a beautiful face. She is an aggressive newspaper reporter with an unusually upbeat approach to life despite an unhappy childhood that included sexual abuse, and a womanhood that included a destructive marriage and the death of a handicapped child. Vickie and Tim became acquainted at the newspaper where they were both employed. He was a makeup man in the composing room.

At first, their acquaintance was the usual "Ha-

ha, how did we get in this business?" repartee common between employees everywhere. Because Vickie worked odd hours, and Tim worked the night shift they began meeting for coffee during their breaks which came at nine, ten or eleven in the evening.

"I remember our first physical contact came after I had been complaining about my neck and shoulders hurting from too much stress. Tim came around behind my chair in the lunchroom and began massaging my neck," Vickie said. "It felt so marvelously wonderful, I began to relax, and the pain seemed to flow right out of me. It was one of the most sensuous neckrubs I had ever had.

"From that night on, our relationship took a very physical form. The next night, I decided to return the favor. I rubbed his hands with my hand lotion. Hands are moving constantly with the cut and paste work of the composing room. I remember Tim saying he thought he had the beginnings of arthritis. I said, 'You can't. You're too young.'

"He got out of his chair, took me in his arms, and kissed me. 'I'm not too young to be in love with you,' he said. I was floored, simply floored. I told him we'd have to talk about it, but it wasn't too long before we were sleeping together, first at his apartment, then at my home.

"It was quite a shock the day I realized that his son was a year younger than my oldest grandchild. I knew there was a difference in our ages, but I didn't realize that 32 and 47 could make that much difference. I tried to point this out to him, but he wouldn't listen.

"We discussed moving in together, and we did live together for three weeks when I was injured in a car accident. He took care of me better than my mother would have.

"We now live in separate apartments, but he wants to be together constantly. I'm beginning to pull away from the relationship, but he clings to me as if I were his mother. In a way, maybe I am. There's nothing he wouldn't do to please me, but his adoration takes such possessive forms.

"I'm smothered. He's jealous of everything I do. To him a reporter's life is glamorous. To me it's a job, slogging through mud or cold or nasty people to get the story you need. There's very little glamour attached to daily newspaper reporting.

"I would like to get away from Tim, but he begs and pleads with me not to leave him. There are times when I feel as if I'm a young mother again with a toddler hanging on my leg. I really don't know what to do.

"I'd have to tell your ladies, don't get mixed up with a younger man unless you're prepared to be his mother as well as his lover."

Sex seems to be a very important draw in the older woman/younger man relationship.

"I'd forgotten what it was like to be made love to several times a night," said a delighted Vickie when her love affair with Tim was in the basic lust stage.

Remember Nona, the vivacious woman who loves to play the personal ad game because of the spicy challenge the game offers? In placing and answering personal ads, Nona has had several affairs with younger men.

"I remember Walt so very well," Nona said. "He

answered my ad that stated that a mid-life woman
wanted fun and companionship. When his letter re-
vealed that he was younger than my son, I wanted to
break off the correspondence, but the letters began arriving even faster. Soon, I agreed to meet Walt. We met
for cocktails and went on to a concert. Our cultural
interests were so much alike. One of our greatest thrills
was to attend 'First Thursdays' in Portland where I live.
On the first Thursday of every month, art galleries in
Old Town are open. Everyone meets first for wine and a
grazing supper of appetizers, then we all visit the galleries, drinking wine and walking from shop to shop. It
is absolute bliss for me to be able to talk art with people.
Because Walt was an art student, it was doubly fascinating."

After about six weeks of dating, Nona and Walt
were sitting and sipping wine before a First Thursday
evening.

"I remember it so well. He was looking at me, and I
said, 'What are you thinking about?' and he said, 'I'm
thinking I'd like to kiss you.' I said, 'So go ahead and do
it.' He did, and it was a nice soft kiss. I enjoyed it, but
when Walt said, 'I'd rather go to bed with you tonight
instead of looking at art,' I thought I'd better call a halt. I
answered, 'Let's go ahead to the galleries, and you go
home and think about it. I'm old enough to be your
mother. If you still want to by the end of the week, you
let me know.' "

Walt thought it over and decided it was the right
thing to do. A week later, he was on Nona's doorstep,
and the two began a close relationship that very night.

"There is a certain sophisticated edge an older woman can bring to a younger man's love live, a special dimension that adds spice to a young man's life," Nona said. "I'm a teacher by heart, and to teach Walt the different steps it takes to please a woman gave us both great pleasure. In time, the relationship ended. There was really no place for it to go, but while it lasted, we both benefited."

Alyse had a chance to date a younger man, but decided it wasn't for her. A social worker, Alyse often works with crime victims in her city. When a sheriff's deputy began to hang around when she was in the courthouse, she was definitely intrigued.

"There's something about young law enforcement officers. They are incredibly sexy in their uniforms. They're so take-charge and macho, they really turn me on. So, I'm still wondering why I didn't go out with Blake when he asked me. God, he was gorgeous, but he scared me to death. I am 48 years old, and he was 27.

"You know how sometimes, and I wish it were more often, an inner voice tells you when something is not right. Well, my inner voice was working, and it told me, 'Whoa, girl, this boy is not for you. He has the power to hurt you.' I am coming down off a disastrous divorce, and I don't need any more pain. I declined his invitation, but I have to tell you now, when I watch him swagger down the hall in that uniform, I think I made a mistake. No, I don't. I know I was right, but not having an affair with Blake will be something I'll regret for years."

Because of the pain Alyse suffered in her marriage relationship, she is thrice careful about herself.

"I've dated men since my divorce, but it's never been quite right. Guess it's that inner voice again telling me to back off. If it doesn't feel right, it doesn't feel right.

"I guess my voice was speaking to me when I saw Blake and a young female dispatcher teasing and talking when I walked into the office. They were so young, and it made me feel so old. That's when I knew I could never get caught in a young man-older woman relationship. Never, never."

Although all women agreed that sex with a younger man is great, other drawbacks make the relationship less than rewarding.

Here are some minuses from grandmothers who have been involved with younger men:

(1) Stamina — or lack thereof. Most women said they simply couldn't keep up with a younger man in the way of activities outside of bed. "As you physically age, you can't deny the fact that your body has more aches and pains," said one grandmother of 48, who balked at downhill skiing.

(2) Jaded outlook. What an awful word, said the grandmother who told me of this minus, "But it's the only word that describes how I feel when I'm with David. Whatever he feels or discovers, I've already done it before; incredible but true. He is beginning to appear pretty naïve to me."

(3) Physical appearance. "I have to work too hard to keep up," said Ellie, a pretty woman of 48. "I look great for 48, but my fellow is 39, and I just don't feel like competing on looks with the girls in his office who are

in their twenties and thirties. I feel like Maggie in Rod Stewart's song. The morning light really shows my age, and I'm getting too tired to care."

(4) Money. He's on his way up, and you're already there. We will discuss this in the "When Money Is the Problem" chapter, but the situation takes on an entirely different meaning when you're older and richer. "I'm not sure I want to provide a 31-year-old with security," said K. T., a pretty blonde in her mid-forties.

(5) Immature. Like it or not, younger men are more immature than an older, wiser woman who has experienced life by marrying and bearing children. It makes no difference as to who has more education.

(6) Boring. "Lord forgive me for saying this, but guys in their thirties bore me even if they have master degrees," said Kay. She just broke off an affair with a 37-year-old who is only four years older than Kay's oldest son.

Vickie, who is now in the process of shedding Tim, says, "Let's face the facts. I'm of the age where I want a man who has his career and finances in hand. I have leisure time to enjoy life now, and I don't want a man looking entirely to me for his guidance, sustenance and entertainment."

The older woman/younger man relationship is a dating aspect that became more fairly common during the 1980s. Why are more and more younger men seeking out the older woman?

Alyse, who has a degree in psychology, said she believes young men are attracted to older women because of the energy older women give off.

"When women are in their forties, they are never

going to be any better sexually," Alyse said. "They look great, usually look 30-ish, and are at the the prime, the peak, of their sensuous selves. They give off an aura of bright power. A younger man senses this, and is powerfully attracted to such a woman.

"I think a woman in her forties and a man in his twenties are just about right, sexually, for each other. Women of this age have the time and the desire to just play. They're not anxious about marriage, and they've already had their children. Sex play is strongly on their mind. Oh, here I am regretting not sleeping with Blake again. I don't want to talk about it any more."

Catherine disagrees. A little sour on the subject, this legal secretary believes that younger men are attracted to older women because they are bewitched by the mother complex.

"Call me cynical," said Catherine, a tall blonde in her early fifties, "but I think young guys who go for older women are acting out their fantasies about sleeping with their mothers. Thank you, but no thank you. I have sons of my own, and I don't want to think about them sleeping with a woman my age. It's distasteful."

Vernie, a 46-year old, said, "My young lover, Kirk, once told me that it was so much easier to trust an older woman; she wouldn't lie to you or cheat on you like a younger woman. It was sort of a back-handed compliment, as if I was so grateful I wouldn't do anything to jeopardize the relationship. It made me look at him in a different way, and I didn't like him quite so much after that."

She broke with Kirk, and is now seeing a man in his sixties. "I don't have to work so hard at this relation-

ship. I know Sam won't lie to me or cheat on me, and I
trust him. I sound just like Kirk, don't I? It's all relevant."

One sophisticated woman in her late forties said, "I
have this imaginary line I draw. If a guy is five years
younger, it's no problem. If he's ten years younger, I
back off and really think it over. If he's fifteen or more
years younger, I just don't get involved. I look down
the line and see myself in my sixties trying to keep pace
with a guy in his forties, and it makes me tired to think
about it. Who wants to go to bed with makeup on? A
constant struggle to keep young is a hassle and, in
consequence, makes a woman look older. The less
stress, the happier and younger a woman is going to
look."

Norma Slover, a private counselor in Salem, Oregon, said she thinks that younger men are attracted to
older women because of the maternal and mature stabil-
ity the relationship offers.

"Occasionally it is an act of rebelliousness on the
part of the young man, like dating someone from another culture or race," she said. "It gives them a sense of
one-upmanship with their peers."

So there you have the private and professional
opinions. Although there are no absolutes in the May/
December romances of men and women, the general
consensus among the grandmothers interviewed was:
"Young men are a great place to visit, but you wouldn't
want to live there."

CHAPTER 12

THE DELICATE TOUCH

When Money Is a Problem

No one really likes to talk about money unless money happens to be a personal obsession. Even devoted couples, who can sit down and dissect their relationship in order to make it better, find it difficult to discuss how to handle financial inequities.

As recently as fifteen years ago, dating money wouldn't have been a problem. Men paid—it was as simple as that. However, the rules have changed. Nowadays, when a mid-life couple begins dating, the question of who pays for what is delicately skirted.

The variations of who's got what breaks down into three categories. Simply defined, they are:

(1) The bucks are evenly divided.
(2) He's got the bucks
(3) She's got the bucks.

Where the couple is relatively equal in worth, the finances of dating should be equally shared. A tactful way to handle the matter is: If the event happens to be the guy's idea, then he pays. If the woman tenders the invitation, she can say easily, "This one's on me."

There should be no problem here unless basic money values differ greatly. Bluntly put, you have problems if one is a tightwad and one is a spendthrift, in varying degrees, of course.

In a previous chapter we talked about danger signals, one of them being how a man spends his money. The subject was outlined briefly, so let's go into it more fully here. There is a difference between:

(1) Careful. If a man's money was hard-come by, he is apt to be more watchful of how it is spent. This man will not scrimp on you, but he may have different ideas of where the money should go. He will not bat an eye at a state-of-the-art television set in his home, but he may scream like a wounded panther at a dinner-for-two bill that exceeds $50.

Men who are careful about money are OK guys, although it may take a little negotiating to set guidelines as to who pays for what entertainment costs. If you consider a dinner à deux at the city's fanciest French bistro an especial treat, make it just that. Your treat. When he gets to know what you like that he can provide, you'll be rewarded in other ways by this careful thoughtful man.

(2) Frugal. Parsimonious might be an alternative word choice here. If you latch onto a frugal sweetie, he will be very conservative in money management. You will find no state-of-the-art television in his dwelling,

just a TV in working order. When it comes to boy toys, his will be practical medium-priced gadgets because this fellow is a "Why spend more?" soul who can happily get by on whatever works. He loves sales, all kinds—store sales, estate sales and going-out-of business sales. This sweetheart is out to save a buck, and you can't really fault him. If frugal is all right with you because you, too, like to buy cheap, fix up, and make-do, then terrific. Whatever works for you two.

If it's a problem because you opt for the top line in whatever you like, and this includes entertainment, perhaps you have a slight problem about values. Pay attention, and you can learn from this frugal fellow who likes to know where every dollar goes. These guys are definitely keepers, although they occasionally may make you rip your hair out.

(3) El Cheapo. Alternative words: Miserly, mean. Not good, right? Right. Men who are stingy with money are often stingy in their emotions, but this trait doesn't mean they will be stingy in their demands from you. They want everything you have to give, but they don't want to pay back in kind. They carry huge books of coupons in their car, and if you go to dinner, you go on a "two-fer" the price of one. You spend hours in a quick lube shop so he can save $1.50 on changing his oil. In a lounge, you stop drinking the instant happy hour is over.

Then there is a Dr. Jekyll/Mr. Hyde type of stingy man. He may be devotedly in love with a woman, and be happy to give her his name, loyalty and faithfulness, then go totally berserk about spending HIS money.

A case comes to mind about a physician once married to a friend of mine. A week after their wedding, she purchased him some new underwear, his being on the hole-filled, tacky side. He went totally nutso. Smashing glasses, kicking over furniture, and shouting that she was a spendthrift. All this from a man who had taken her to a spendy Club Med for their honeymoon. The marriage went downhill from that first terrible display of temper. Although, as a doctor, he made plenty, he had a terrible obsession about money which hadn't surfaced in the courtship stages. They were divorced eight months later, and she is still shaken by the experience.

El Cheapos usually aren't that difficult to spot. A garden variety miser is one who you know has funds, but hates to part with a penny. These guys start young. I remember a guy in high school who always arranged to meet me inside the movie, not by the ticket booth. During a movie he would say he had to go to the restroom, I'd go out later, and there he'd be standing in a corner swilling coke and stuffing down popcorn. Naturally, I wasn't offered a treat because his allowance was more important to him than I was.

These guys grow up to scrimp needlessly on both necessities and entertainment. When they deal with friends, they aren't above a bit of cheating when it comes to money. They're the ones who have to go to the restroom when it's time to pay the bill or go back to the table and pick up half the tip they've left for the waitress (you think I made this up?). If there's a way to manipulate a bill, whether it be for dry cleaning or income taxes, these guys are always working the angles. They want everything entitled to them—and then some.

Unless you're a Ms. Miser who can clip coupons

with him, don't fall in love with El Cheapo; he's not worth the pain.

A really bad sign: If he has to go to the back yard with a shovel instead of to a bank for cash, watch out. You really have an odd one.

There you have the three. When you think that your man is a bit careful with a buck, read over this chapter and pin him down as to type. Always remember, a wise man concerns himself with money matters; a foolish man makes money his life's concern.

What about Money Problem No. 2? The guy has the bucks and you have little or none. Many women would shrug, and say "What's to complain? Whoopee! He's got, I ain't got, so give a little, honey. Give me a lifestyle to which I can become accustomed."

Mr. Gotrocks' behavior can fall into three categories:

(1) He's a perfect gentleman and wouldn't consider letting you spend your hard-earned cash on anything for him. He will happily take what you give him—and we'll talk about that in a moment—and consider himself lucky.

These are the most wonderful sweethearts in the world. If you're lucky enough to find one, don't abuse his generosity. It's not necessary to make up for a lifetime of deprivation by making your caring darling pony up for things you ordinarily wouldn't buy yourself.

I knew a lady who did that, and now when her sweetheart looks at her, it is with disgust for the materialistic woman she has become and regret for the sweet lady she was.

(2) He's a mouth like Mickey. Mickey is a really nice guy. If you need anything, he's there before you ask,

but when it comes to male/female relationships, he is one of the least compassionate guys I know. Mickey has literally put his money where his mouth is and his mouth is always in gear. He's too often heard making disparaging remarks about his wife's lack of income, even though it was he who made her quit her job when they married.

Although he showers his wife with gifts and takes her to the nicest places, he's not Mr. Adorable when he opens his mouth. One of his favorite jokes, always voiced when there are many people around, is "Well, I love my Dollie, even if she is financially impotent."

She smiles a pained little smile, laughs a nervous little laugh, and tells her friends, "He isn't like that when we're alone. He is perfectly wonderful to me."

She has a problem because Mickey Mouth most definitely has a problem. For reasons known only to him—he'll probably try and blame it on his mother—Mickey must build himself up in public. If that means tearing his sweetheart down, then she'd better get used to it.

Another Mickey classic is his line—heard too many times by his friends—that he lives by the Golden Rule. "He who makes the gold, makes the rules." He thinks he's working the crowd for a laugh, but is that what he is really doing? Is there a deep-rooted problem in this marriage?

If this couple's relationship is ever to progress to a happy marriage, then she had best speak out and tell Mouth that his statements are not acceptable. If it means leaving him, then so be it. If a man really loves you, he will listen and learn. If he doesn't, you haven't lost anything worth keeping. You'll leave with your pride and spirit intact, and that's what really matters.

You may be a saint and decide that Mickey Mouth has so many good qualities you'll be able to overlook the cracks about being the one with the gold. Be careful. Marriage always accentuates the negatives.

(3) This last guy is a royal bore. Brad Brag's got money, and he'll gladly tell you exactly how he got his money. He's rich, rich, rich, and he's clever, clever, clever—and he'll never let you forget it for one moment.

This guy may pay your way now, but in the future, you'll pay in ways you didn't dream possible. Now think about it. All that money isn't really worth it, is it? If you think it is, then go for it. There's another old adage I'll mention: If you marry for money, you'll never work any harder.

With Mickey Mouth and Brad Brag, being the one with the loot is their way of expressing the traditional chauvinistic method of control. I doubt if these men could handle a woman who is as monetarily successful as they were, especially if the woman makes the money herself. Successful women terrify these guys. Their wallets are attached to their testicles and they feel castrated unless they can feel their wallet in their back pocket. And their foot on the necks of their darlings.

Despite their surface generosity, men like these two can be nearly impossible to live with. They could be really nice guys if, somewhere along the way, money hadn't warped their reason.

Hopefully, if he's got the money you've found a Number One. He is a prince among fellows. Cherish this jewel for the precious person that he is. How can you make your value clear to him? Your thoughts take the line of, "This isn't really fair." He gives and I take. What can I do about it?''

Your choices are many, but zero right in on the most important gift you have: Your talent as a loving and nurturing woman.

He may be able to wine and dine you at a five-star restaurant, but who's going to make him chicken soup when he's got a scratchy throat and the night is cold? He may drive a Mercedes, but who's going to build him up when the world is beating him down? He may be front row center on opening night, but who's going to be there when the spotlights dim?

You know the answers to all three questions, and you, of course, are the answer. You will do all these things, not as payment, but because you sincerely love this man and want to give him all that he deserves.

Let's talk about the spendthrift. He plays grasshopper to your ant. Life with him is here, there and everywhere. Nothing is too good for his honey, although you know his income is just about average. A night out with Joe Blow is credit cards all the way. No house wine, no balcony seats, no stay-at-home dinners when there's the big, wide world out there to play in.

Soon, you'll notice that Joe Blow is in a real mood. He's so down that not even you can lift him up. When you're at his place, you notice a stack of unpaid bills a foot high on his desk.

Don't peek. There's no need to. You know that Joe has overspent again. You may love him, but if you don't have the money to bail him out when he's overdosed on plastic, I'd advise steering clear.

Joe Blows are rarely cured. The moment a crisis is

past, he'll run wild again. The luxurious presents he
brings begin to sicken you because you know there's a
terrible sickness in poor Joe. He may not be hooked on
liquor, dope or gambling, but his overspending is just
as much an addiction, and you don't need a man who
does anything to excess.

Now we come to the last and touchiest problem
with mid-life dating. You have more money than he
does.

The reasons for this are varied. You are a widow
and have been left a large insurance benefit plus proper-
ties. You are a divorcée, and your settlement looms as
large as the World Trade Center between you and your
intended sweetie. You're a silver-spooned gal because
your family has always had money. You've forged
ahead in your field and outdistanced all the others.

No matter how you got the money, you shouldn't
let it cause a problem if you want to make a relationship
work. From a savvy stockbroker with money comes
these pearls of wisdom:

"You must make every effort at building up his
self-esteem. Find out what he is good at and utilize his
talents. My hobby is buying and selling Victorian-era
homes, and in my leisure I love to get down and do
much of the work myself, but there are some things I
really don't know about. Plumbing, electrical things,
and structural defects are not in my line. I'm the wood
finisher, the fresh paint and pretty wallpaper person.

"Wes is a clever fixer-upper. He was a supply ser-
geant in the Army, and he knows a little bit about a lot
of things. There is virtually nothing Wes can't fix. He
has taken such a load off me in this department, and I
constantly tell him how much it means to me.

"When we were dating, entertainment became a problem because, being in the business that I am in, the functions are costly, and I often have to take clients out to dinner. I solved this problem by looking him in the eye when he came to pick me up, handing him the cash to take care of the evening, and saying firmly, 'Now this is business, and it has nothing to do with us.'

"He balked a little at first, but gradually I got him to see the reasoning behind it. It was my business to entertain, and there was no reason for him to think he had to pay for it. I asked him 'If the shoe was on the other foot, would you feel bad if I didn't pay for your business duties?' This rationale made sense, and we didn't have any trouble after that."

Vacations were a tougher matter for this couple who liked to travel.

"I just had to speak frankly, and say, 'We both love to travel, and I have the money to pay for it. Let's go and enjoy ourselves."

The bottom line, this woman said, is to build up the self-esteem and talents of your beloved so that he never feels as if he is not giving enough to the relationship.

Isn't this exactly the way of handling the "He's got/ She doesn't" problem we talked about earlier in this chapter? If the situation is approached with finesse and each partner is allowed to contribute what he or she best contributes, the relationship will work.

I can't write a chapter on money and its effect on a relationship without mentioning the leeches. If you are a woman of substance, you know they exist. You find them everywhere you turn. These parasitic lugs can be found in any level of society, but they most often cluster around the big money spots where single mid-life women with a bankroll often gather.

It's easy for a woman to be taken in by leeches because they generally come in such pretty packages, and they do so well those things they do. These men make their living by knowing exactly how and when to push the right buttons of a mid-life woman.

Here's a quick quiz to check for parasites in your life:

(1) Did you find him or did he find you? Did he appear from out of nowhere and suddenly begin dancing at your elbow, ready to offer his services wherever you might need him?

(2) Are his credentials good? Is he responsibly employed, no matter how lowly the position, or is he always on the fringe of employment? Always waiting for the phone call that will boost him into the upper incomes?

(3) Do you have mutual friends who will tell you frankly what they know about this man?

(4) Has he come to accept your largesse as his rightful due?

(5) Has he approached you with any get-rich-quick schemes? Gold mines in Peru? Uranium mines in Paraguay? Oil in an obscure lake in uppermost Kenya?

(6) Do hard luck tales surface? He's had to put a mother in a rest home, and he can't put her in just any rest home. His sister has terminal cancer. His brother has a brain tumor. Just any little bit would help.

(7) Has he taken too readily to the good life? If you

want him on an afternoon, can you usually find him at your country club, signing your private number on the drink checks during his gin game?

(8) When you've handed over the money so badly needed, does his attention quickly shift from you to other interests?

The last is a sure cure, said a wealthy woman I know.

"The minute I handed over the needed cash, Rick wasn't quite so available, I noticed. When he needed some more, he was mine twenty-four hours a day again."

Maybe you are one of those women whose turn-on is to control the purse strings. You will always find some man willing to play your game. But if you are what your money has made you, others will find the workmanship shoddy.

The problem of money need not be insurmountable if you two discuss it openly.

One last warning: Many men consider themselves far better at handling money than are women. The truth is that most women are quite competent in handling their finances. If you know yourself to be a capable manager, don't be bullied into corners where money is concerned.

CHAPTER 13

WHEN A NEW WOMAN MEETS A GOOD OLD BOY

Let's talk about grandmothers and the feminist movement. I can just hear some of you now. "But, Gloria, I'm not one of those women." Stick with me, ladies. Whether you realize it or not, the feminist viewpoint does most definitely fit right into our scheme of getting you out into the mainstream.

You may not think you're a feminist, but, well, let's hear from Martha and Virginia.

In 1973, these women, wives and mothers in their mid-forties, attended the first feminist conference held in their state. Suited, gloved, and filled with enthusiasm, the two drove to the conference center in the mountains.

As they entered the center, Martha and Virginia, both concerned women, became increasingly concerned about what they saw happening around them.

"Martha and I were were interested in obtaining equal pay for women," Virginia said. "We realized that there had to be a better daycare system to allow welfare mothers to get off welfare. Although neither of us would have had an abortion, we would never deny another woman the right of choice for her own body. And we knew that to get these things done, we'd have to have more women in government."

But as they were registering, their eyes were opened to an unexpected situation. Some of the participants had other matters on their minds.

"There was a disturbing element," Martha said. "A group of angry women, army-booted and wearing fatigues, were attempting to take over the conference, and by sheer noise level they were succeeding. Their language was obscene, and they were hanging up hand-printed advertisements asking for liberal minded swinging partners for the evening.

"At one point, during a goals-setting workshop, one hostile woman took the stage and screamed, 'Any woman who doesn't have a woman lover doesn't love women.' To second that thought, her friend yelled, 'A woman without a man is like a fish without a bicycle!' It was obvious they weren't as concerned about the inequities in the system as they were in achieving acceptance of their sexual persuasion.

"I'd never thought of myself as a prude. Sex

doesn't embarrass me, but I don't talk about it. It's a private thing. I tried, I really tried to feel what these women were feeling, but it seemed to have nothing to do with getting our views before the world. It certainly didn't seem the way to get ahead in a male-oriented society," Martha said quietly.

Martha and Virginia were dismayed, disappointed, and completely turned off after one woman took over a workshop on government. She declared that all women should vote for all women candidates, and not vote unless there was a woman to vote for.

Virginia and Martha had had enough. Along with many other women they drove home and tried to forget the feminist movement. However, they continued to work quietly for what they believed in.

For these women, the verdict was in: Being a feminist was the same as being a lesbian, and they wanted no part in it.

"It wasn't that I was against lesbianism," Virginia said. "Everyone to their own tastes, but why didn't they just shut up and get on to more important matters?"

Martha and Virginia are typical and traditional women of the early 1970s. They were open-minded enough to look into the feminist movement, but they didn't like what they saw, so they retreated. And yet, these two women have been pursuing real feminist ideals for years.

Martha, an office supervisor at a cannery, went to bat for a young employee who was being sexually harassed by an older male worker. After the belt manager denied the young woman's charges, Martha went to the

cannery administrators, told them what was going on
and gathered witnesses. She insisted on arbitration at
the labor table about the problem, which had been long-
standing in the cannery.

Virginia, whose children had graduated from high
school and gone off to college, was a moderately well-
off widow. By the late 1970s, she had become bored
with duplicate bridge and golfing. She volunteered to
staff a women's crisis center hotline phone. She became
concerned about the problems of battered and abused
women and children. She was inspired to finish college
to get her degree in sociology, and she is now a counsel-
or for the same center.

Both women are members of the Business and Professional Women and the League of Women Voters.
With other league members, they worked to get a female judge appointed to the traditionally all-male su-
preme court of their state. Both women are the first to
answer the call if volunteers are needed.

Martha and Virginia live and breathe what the feminist movement is all about, yet both would deny they
are feminists in the sense of what the word meant to
them in the early seventies.

"We just believe in doing what is right," they say.

Doing what is right and working for the feminist
cause are synonomous, but convincing some women in
mid-age brackets of this is difficult.

What they've not stopped to discover is that today's feminist movement, although no less determined
than the earlier version, has adopted a calmer, more
rational approach to problems. Also, many men have
joined in the cause. Feminist issues of yesterday have

become public issues of today, and federal, state, county and city governments have awakened to the fact that affordable day care is effective in getting women off the welfare rolls and into the mainstream of business.

Both women are now in their mid-sixties and single. Virginia has not remarried, and in 1983 Martha finally found the courage to divorce a husband who refused to admit to and be treated for alcoholism. He has since remarried and is currently, Martha heard, making his new wife just as miserable as he made her.

Through a class in writing that was offered at their senior center, Martha and Virginia became active in center activities. When they reentered the male-female social scene, the feminist viewpoint unexpectedly entered their lives.

Martha began thinking of dating the instant she spied Les at the center. There was an immediate attraction between petite and classy Martha and big, brawny Les, who had owned a trucking firm. He kept in shape by jogging and lifting weights when he wasn't fishing and hunting.

A jolly sort, Les was the life of the party at the Saturday afternoon tea dances held at the center. The single women, who outnumbered the single men nearly three to one, clustered around Big Les like bees around the honeycomb. Martha was flattered when he began to single her out for the tricky step numbers.

"I was amazed at how good it felt to be held and to have a big strong body to hold," said Martha, who hadn't held or been held for more years than she cared to remember. "I thought I was beyond all that."

However, there was a quality about Les that made

Martha uneasy. He seemed a bit demeaning in his jokes about women. Like a cock in a henhouse, Les ruled the roost in the tea dance coterie and called every woman, "honey" or "pretty little thing" or "sugar." Les often recounted adventures that had him in control over women who, according to his stories, were too weak or too simple to have solved the problems themselves.

"I've heard his story about the 'little lady' who had a flat and didn't know her jack from a fire extinguisher three times already," Martha said. Naturally, in Les's version of the story, he came to the rescue and saved this "poor little darlin' " from the big bad world.

When Les invited Martha for dinner and a movie, she was intrigued by his masculinity, but anxious about his "good ol' boyism." What Martha didn't realize was that although she thought she'd divorced herself from the feminist movement, the philosophy had taken root in her mind. She had become feminist in her ideas as to how a man-woman relationship should work.

For eight years, Martha had been living and managing on her own. She tended her yard, took a class in auto repair, and could replace her own spark plugs. Checkbooks didn't frighten her, and her finances were in good shape. She even took a little flyer in the stock market and doubled her small investment.

At 64, Martha is a true woman of the nineties. She can live very well without a man to take care of her.

But that doesn't mean she doesn't want a man. She wants a man with whom she can be friend, lover and companion. She certainly doesn't need a man who builds up his own ego by tearing down a woman's esteem.

"When I got the invitation, I was all fluttery," she said. "I thought it silly of me, but I was really looking forward to dinner with Les. I just hoped he wouldn't pull the 'big strong me, poor little you' act. He didn't need to with me. I liked him without being hit over the head that he was stronger and believed he was smarter than any woman.

"I was torn. What shall I do, I kept asking myself."

A man is as complex as a woman, and often, he will say or do what he thinks is expected of him. Don't forget that a man in his sixties grew up in an era when women were to be taken care of, protected from life and cherished. That certainly is not all bad because most women like to be taken care of, protected and cherished. The difference is in the perception of what caring, protecting and cherishing actually entail.

Men in their sixties and seventies were programmed into the "man's work, woman's work" pre-World War II syndrome. They are only too content to perpetuate the syndrome because they believe this to be "the natural order of things." Because many of these men are still lumbering through the Dinosaur Age of male-female relationships, it's difficult for the darlings to let go of the ideas. After all, why should they?

For instance, a man who can't conceive of letting his wife run the power lawn mower doesn't blink an eye at letting her tote three loads of wash down to the utility room, wash and fold the clothes, then haul them back up the stairs to put them away. While he may make arrangements for the car to be repaired, he thinks nothing of having his wife drop the car off and pick it up. She is expected not only to pick up the car, but also

to do the marketing, stop by the cleaners, come home
and prepare the evening meal, and clean up afterward.
And all this after she's worked an eight-hour day in an
office.

The inequity of this rolls right over his head because, in his mind, he has fulfilled his male role by
making the appointment and dickering with the mechanic about the price.

Of course, for this to happen, a woman has to
consent. That's where Martha decided that if Les played
good ol' boy to the hilt, she would simply say,
"Enough."

With this decision made, she relaxed and went to
dinner with Les. He was a perfect escort, arriving with a
bouquet of flowers at her front door. He had made
reservations at one of their city's nicest restaurants, and
they had no trouble making conversation over their
dinner and after the movie.

"We found we had many things in common," Martha said. "Love of our children and grandchildren, a
love for the ocean, and a desire to keep the environment
clean and protected. And he never once belittled the
weaknesses of women."

What Martha discovered is that you cannot always
judge a book by its cover, if you'll pardon the cliche.
Les's "Well, shucks, Sugar . . . " manner at the Center
dances disguised an educated, thinking man. He didn't
even realize he was demeaning women with his superior male attitude, because he'd grown up in the Texas
oilfields. All the men he knew talked and acted just as
he did, and their women fluttered when they preened
because that was the way things were done in those
good old days.

Martha's quick-witted replies to Les's sallies made him roar with laughter. They also made him take a second look because, in his own way, he was just as quick-witted.

Now, he has only to throw out a "Now, Sugar . . ." to get a glint in her brown eyes, a glint that tells him, "I really like you, but don't you 'Sugar' me."

Virginia had a much tougher problem, although many women would contend that the problem was a blessing. Virginia began dating LaMar five years ago. He was a dapper man in his early seventies, physically fit in body, fiscally fit in bankroll.

They met at a golf tournament. Virginia had dropped golf when she began volunteering at the crisis center, but decided to pick it up again because it's a great stress reliever and her job was filled with trauma. She and LaMar were paired for the couples golf tournament on a public golf course. She laughs about this now, saying, "I still can't figure how out why this big chief let himself be talked into a tournament outside his own particular reservation."

The dapper LaMar, a Southern gentleman to the fingertips, was immediately attracted to Virginia's cool blonde good looks and trim figure. Virginia liked LaMar's consideration, his looks, and his knowledge of world affairs. She found that you can cover a lot of topics during an eighteen-hole tournament. LaMar was a little opinionated, but what the heck? Virginia thought, he was just trying to impress her.

He called the following week, and Virginia asked him to one of the Saturday afternoon tea dances at the senior center. He accepted readily, and although she didn't realize he didn't cotton to her chums at the center, he certainly cottoned to Virginia. He responded with an invitation for dinner. She readily accepted the invitation, then a second, and a third.

On the third date LaMar's built-in prejudices began to creep into the conversation. He'd made, he declared, his last visit to the center. They were really nice people, he said, with a wave of his well-manicured hand, but, "Well, they're not really our kind, are they?

"I knew from the moment we met that we were on the same educational and social status level," he confided over wine at dinner one evening.

Virginia countered this kind of talk with talk of her work with battered and abused women. A look of horror came over his face, and he asked, "How can you stand to be around people like that?"

Then he went on to a long story about how an Oriental family had tried to get into the club, but they were blackballed. "We couldn't let down our standards," he told Virginia.

She made up her mind never to see this man again, but at the evening's close, he invited her to a friend's beach home for a weekend of tennis, golf and socializing. He made it clear that there would be no pressure for physical intimacy, and she would have her own room.

"It just wouldn't do any other way," he said, pressing her hand and reassuring her that it wasn't because he didn't think she was attractive. "We just have to mind our manners."

Well, that's not bad, Virginia thought, weakening. And a weekend of fun and leisure at a plush coast hideway sounded good. So she accepted, and although she found LaMar's friends a tad stodgy with a rather callous "us against the them" attitude about the ills of the world, she had to admit that she did have a good time.

What was not to like? The food was delicious, a servant did the washing up; there was absolutely nothing to think about but having a good time. Virginia and LaMar went from the links to lunch al fresco at the lodge. The rest of the afternoon she lay in a chaise lounge, reading a favorite P.D. James mystery. The only thought that crossed her mind was what she would wear to dinner that evening. She had never been so coddled in her life. Her late husband, Roger, had been a workaholic who rarely gave a thought beyond his profit margin.

Gradually, Virginia was lured into the lush life offered by LaMar, who was a perfect companion with much to offer in the way of "having fun." When he did decide to stop "minding his manners," the sex, while not dynamite, was pleasant.

LaMar suggested marriage in the late summer, followed by a long honeyoon in Europe with a group of his friends. His proposal went something along the lines of, "We go together like ham and eggs, darling. We like the same things, like the same life, and have the same values."

What woman could resist a chance at love and life on a grand scale?

Bur Virginia wasn't sure about having the same values. There was a discomforting prickle when she attempted to tell of a particularly moving case of a black

teenage prostitute who had been battered and bruised
by a boyfriend after he'd found she was pregnant. The
girl had fled to the crisis shelter, and Virginia was trying
to help her find a job.

LaMar asked, disparagingly, why should Virginia
worry about the case. "Blacks can't pull themselves up
because they don't know what up is," he said.

Then he reached over, patted her hand and said,
"Don't worry, sweetheart, after we're married, you'll
never ever again have to trouble your head about a
black woman who can't keep her legs together," he
said.

At those words, Virginia's first impulse was to rip
off her one-and-a-half-carat diamond ring and throw it
across the table. Then common sense, or perhaps sheer
survival, took over.

Marriage. A wedding trip to Europe. No more slogging through the winter rain to meet with women who
didn't seem to make much progress in bettering themselves, who oftimes defended their abusers, and sometimes struck out at the counselor who was trying to
help. A child's storybook dream of romance with marriage the final prize. Just a life of drifting, a life of ease
with no pain, no strain.

But would she be content?

She confided her fears to Martha. "I just don't live
in an insulated bubble of pleasure. If women don't get
out and try to make a better world, what's going to
happen to us? Last week at a club social, a man said to
me, 'This country isn't ready for a woman president.' I
said, 'It's overdue. How could a woman make our
world any worse than it is?' "

The man, one of LaMar's golf partners, stomped off

to the men's bar at the club—the one where women aren't permitted until 6 P.M. His wife patted Virginia's hand and said, "Darling, why do you say things like this? It upsets our fellows."

Why indeed? Because Virginia and Martha are women whose eyes have been opened to the world. If you'd told them at that long-ago feminist conference that their own lives would be touched by feminist ideals, they'd have hooted in disbelief.

But every woman, unless she lives her life in a vacuum as an appendage to her husband's ego, has had her life touched in some way by feminist causes. For many, it has changed forever their way of looking at things.

If you are reading this chapter waiting for me to provide you with an answer to what happens when a new woman falls in love with a good old boy, I'm sorry, ladies. There is no pat answer. Each individual problem has its own individual solution.

I can tell you how Martha and Virginia resolved their problems. Martha and Les wed in 1985 and are happily married. When they're not at home gardening and tending their grandchildren, they're on the road with their fifth-wheeler, fishing, rockhounding, and exploring.

Martha's bottom-line decision was that Les was a gentleman in the true meaning of the word. When he dons a Santa Claus suit and trucks down toys and gifts to the children and women at Virginia's shelter, Martha beams with pride. Whenever he goes to a ball game, he generally takes a bunch of neighborhood kids with him.

"He treats me wonderfully, he's thoughtful, and as considerate of my children as he is his own, and I love him. And because he respects me, he grins and shuts up when I give him that 'Cool it, big boy' look," Martha said.

Respect is a key word in any relationship. Martha got real respect from Les, while Virginia, despite surface politeness, got absolutely no respect from LaMar.

When Virginia tried to explain to LaMar how important her job as counselor is to her and how, in her own way, she is confident that she can help women turn their lives around, his reply was that he did not understand why any real lady would get down and work with the lower classes when there are others to do it.

"He listened to me with his ears, but never with his heart," Virginia said.

Virginia gave back the ring she'd privately dubbed "The Rock," and the two parted over a civilized dinner for two—at the club, of course. The women friends Virginia made while with LaMar called her an idealistic idiot of the first order.

She's back in the trenches again, working on an especially difficult case concerning a young mother who is married to a man whom Virginia believes is homicidal. Virginia hasn't played golf in six months, her nails have gone to hell, and dinner is whatever she remembered to put in the crockpot that morning.

Does she miss LaMar and the good life he represented? You bet she does, and there are black nights when she chastizes herself for being the fool of all fools.

"But in the morning, when I'm back at my desk trying to unravel a knotty problem, I know I'm doing what I do best, using the talents God gave me," Virginia said. "I had been a LaMar woman before I finally discovered I was my own woman. I will never again be what a man wants me to be if it goes against my basic instincts and values," Virginia said.

So, ladies, there is no definite answer to the question: What does a New Woman do when she's attracted to a Good Old Boy?

You are the only person who can answer the basic questions, "How does he treat me? Does he respect me as a woman?" And if he doesn't, can you live with that?

CHAPTER 14

LET'S HEAR IT
FROM THE GRANDPAS

From Their Mouths to Your Ears

Many grandmothers haven't a clue as to what grand-fathers want and need when it comes to a rest-of-the-life companion. The best way to discover what's in their minds is to let them tell us.

This input is from typical single grandfathers I've interviewed. They range in age from late forties to mid-eighties with educations spanning from high school diplomas to masters' and Ph.D.s. Financially, these men covered the entire spectrum: from the comfortably wealthy to those struggling between Social Security checks.

These men were perfectly willing to be interviewed

and very definite about what they want. A skeptical editor commented that the requests sound like an ad from a personals column. Some of the grandfathers you'll want to cuddle. Some of the grandfathers—well, you'd love to pinch their little heads off.

I've left off the last names and, in some cases, changed the first names to protect their privacy, but they are alive, well and living more or less happily in the Pacific Northwest.

Gary: An attractive bachelor who owns several auto mechanic's shops. Gary wants "a woman who will pay as much attention to my children as she does her own. I've gone with several women who go overboard trying to make their children happy, but don't make an effort at all to do things for my children.

"I love my kids and they're very important to me. Why can't some women see that?"

Jack: A bachelor in his late forties, Jack has two failed marriages behind him. "I know some of it was my fault, but at this stage of my life, I simply want to be comfortable and happy with a woman who wants to have fun. I don't want a serious commitment. I want to have a good time with a woman who likes sports and travel.

"My days of raising a family are pretty much over. I just want to have fun with a pretty woman who thinks I'm terrific. If that sounds selfish, well, I guess I have the right to say what I want. I've worked long and I've worked hard. It's my turn to be happy."

Nolan: Nolan is a bitter man, but he's willing to try again with a relationship. Divorced many years, he formed a strong attachment with a charming lady he met at a seniors' group. They went steadily for some

months until he began to notice that Betty, his
ladyfriend, spent an inordinate amount of time with a
neighbor she called a good friend. Nolan did a bit of
snooping and found that she and the neighbor had had
an affair which was still more or less going on. Nolan,
an investigative sort, soon discovered that Betty was
using Nolan to take her places where her married lover
would be.

"So all I'm asking is that a woman be up front and
honest with me. No phonies, please. I adhere to strong
Christian principles and Betty nearly broke my heart
with her double dealing.

"I like an attractive, smart, and intelligent woman,
but if she's not honest, then there's no use. I learned my
lesson."

Dick: An active man who's dedicated to his work,
he's had his marriage break up because of his workaholic attitude. Dick says: "I want a woman who loves
her home and will be there waiting for me when I get
home. She's got to be understanding about my work
because a lot of responsibility rests on my shoulders.

"If I don't produce, a lot of people will go down the
drain with me. I know I put work first. I always have,
and I guess I always will.

"She's got to be ready to go when I travel, at home
when I get there. It sounds like a tall order, but it's what
I want and what I need, if I do decide to look for a
mate."

Don: An intelligent and articulate newspaperman
of many years, Don has definite ideas about what he
looks for in a woman.

"I look at the woman's children and her relationship with them. If she and her children are fond of each other, if there are a lot of 'I love you's' and affection between mother and children, then I figure she will be warm and loving with me. If she shows respect for her children, then I believe she will show respect for me.

"And I do like a comfortable relationship with a home-loving woman who's easy and fun to be with."

Mel: He's in his sixties and still looking. "I want a woman to truly like me. I think I could spot a phony pretty quick, but I'm a little gun shy. That old song, 'Stand by Your Man,' sort of sums it up for me. I want her loving and loyal, affectionate and funny, and if she can bake a good apple pie, that's an added plus."

Jerrold: "Hey, I want the cheerleader I never had in high school. Big boobs, lots of blonde hair and good legs, and a bubbly personality. I was a fat nerd in high school and no cheerleader ever dated me.

"I don't know if I'd date a grandmother even though I'm a grandfather. I'm 62 going on 37 and I don't want to slow down until I die." He's a salesman, with one divorce and no plans for marriage, "Just a good time," he says.

Lloyd: He's been widowed since 1982, and is willing to give marriage or a live-in relationship a chance. "What do I look for in a woman? I want a good woman with a good heart, one who will go to church with me, be fun to be with and willing to try something new."

Paul: Recently widowed, Paul still gets tears in his eyes when he talks of his late wife, to whom he was married for forty-nine years.

"I'd like a tall, slim girl. My wife was like that. I

became interested in one lady, and we went out quite a bit when she was diagnosed as having an incurable illness. She dropped me.

"I know it was kind of her to do that, in some ways, but I still feel as if I've been rejected. I'd sure like to find someone who is interested in square dancing."

Phil: An investment analyst, now in his early eighties, Phil has both a bachelor's and master's degree. He has spent fifteen years alone, but would consider remarriage or a good relationship.

"I want someone who is intelligent, who reads and keeps up with what is going on in the community and the world. A woman has to use her mind to stay attractive to a man. I don't like women with closed minds; an inflexibility to ideas and issues not her own denotes, to me, a lack of appreciation for the world around her.

"A woman doesn't have to be beautiful to attract me, but she should be well-groomed and not sloppy fat. All other things being equal, I would certainly choose a woman who kept herself trim and well-groomed over one who would not."

"I'm an ecologist and I want a woman who is interested in helping save this world for our grandchildren."

Shiff: A retired farmer, Shiff is a man's man and loves to be out of doors hunting and fishing.

"I wish I could find a woman who would be interested in doing my kind of things. I'd be glad to do hers, whatever it is, if she would share. So far, most of the ladies I've met are too set in their ways. They don't want to do anything but what they used to do with their dead husbands.

"I met one gal who has never hunted or fished and said she thought she might like it, but didn't I think she was a little too old to learn?

"I told her that no one was too old to learn, but she would never go fishing with me, just wanted me to go to art galleries and concerts. I'm not against those things, but I want a partnership.

"Tell a woman that if she thinks she's too old, then she's not attractive to a man. An older woman with a young woman's attitude toward life is not easy to find."

Ray: This tall and good-looking mechanical engineer, now retired, is a native of Michigan. He is divorced.

"What do I look for? Her legs and her bust. No, don't put that, I'm just kidding.

"Well, she's got to have a good personality, be vivacious and ready to have fun. Good common sense is a wonderful trait in a woman. Well-groomed and a sense of style. I like women who dress well in flattering colors. I'll always give a woman a compliment if she's a good dresser.

"Being badly groomed is a sign of low self-respect. I don't say she's got to be slender, but I don't want anyone fat. That's a lack of discipline."

Earl: A retired accountant, his social life centers around his city's senior citizen group. "Give me a woman who has a good sense of humor and the good sense not to be possessive. I was going with one lady, and she got so possessive of me that she wouldn't let me speak to any other woman around here (a senior center).

"She got to be no fun at all."

Robb: No strings, please, asks this handsome guy in his fifties. He's just coming out of a divorce.

"I've got a new job in a new profession, have a child from my previous marriage who needs me as daddy, and am running a business on the side. I was going with a nice gal but she started pressuring me. I told her to "back off" but she kept pushing, so I dropped her.

"What women need to understand is that dating doesn't have to lead to marriage or a lasting relationship. Sometimes it is just that, dating. Give me a woman who is looking for a good time and I'll show her a good time. Give me a woman who is looking for marriage with every man she dates, and I'll show her the door."

Walter: In his early sixties, Walter is still a hard drinker, hard worker, and hard player.

"I want a woman who appreciates me, loves me and will take care of me. In exchange, I will take care of her, but she's got to put my wants and needs first. I don't mean I want a doormat, but I've got to be Numero Uno in her book. Love, loyalty and sex are what I want, in that order."

Richard: A quiet and shy man, Richard goes to church every Sunday and, during the week, teaches classes in woodworking at the senior center. "It may sound a little old-fashioned, but that's what I am. I want a woman who has high morals and good values. She doesn't have to be real pretty, but I want her to have the same religious beliefs that I have (Richard is a Catholic), and I want a nice family woman who will love me and my children. I don't like fat women, though."

Mayford: An environmentalist outdoorsman, Mayford is in his early sixties. He wants a woman "who will go on hikes with me, dance with me, and do things. I like to get out and do things while I'm able to. Give me a woman who won't whine when her feet get wet and can open a can of beans out on the trail and make them taste like a gourmet feast and I'll be her slave forever."

Crawford: "That's simple to answer," said this man who is still employed part-time at a local cannery. "I want what every man wants. I want a woman to be my best friend, a good lover who is true to me, and one who has the same values about home and family that I do. If she's in a pretty package, that's so much the better."

Stewart: "Well, there's one good way you're gonna know if a lady is a nice person. That's when you watch her behaving to women when there's a man around."

A widower in his seventies, Stew attends regular dances at a senior center. He has this to say, and ladies, pay attention here:

"I go to these dances all the time, and I know there aren't many of us single guys to go around, but some women just behave awful. Why, I've stood right out there on the dance floor and had two women fight over me.

"You tell that to guys, and they'll laugh, but it's not funny. Seems like when some women get lonely, they get mean to other women, like they were competition or something. Some of 'em get real mean eyes. I've read where eyes are mirrors to the soul, well, some of those ladies don't have nice souls. They act all sweet and nice around the guys, then another woman walks up and they turn cold as ice towards that woman.

"Give me a woman who is nice and kind to every-one, just not men."

Lee: A retired state worker, Lee has been widowed for several years.

"I want a woman who is considerate, affectionate, and willing to have fun. After a couple goes out together for some time, I think they should have some time in a home setting. It gives a period of insight into whether or not they will be compatible.

"Take some real time together to get to know each other. Women who rush things worry me. I think two years going together is a good length of time to know each other. You can avoid a lot of problems if you do this, but some women don't seem to realize this."

Loren and Emma. This couple, in their sixties, met at a senior center. They are sublimely happy.

Loren was ready and willing to talk about what attracted him to Emma.

"She is lively, attractive and interested in what's going on around her. She's also got good sense, and she's intelligent. She plays a heck of a good game of golf.

"First time I saw her, I liked her, she was so lively and full of fun. Second time, I just happened, ha ha, to have my golf clubs in the car, and I asked her out to play golf. We liked each other right off.

"One of the main things is her good sense of humor. An insurance guy told me the other day that having a good sense of humor can keep a person out of a nursing home six or seven years longer than those without a good sense of humor.

"Isn't that amazing? Well, Emma and I don't have any plans for a nursing home. We're too busy having fun."

That is absolutely the best thing two people of "that certain age" can be doing with one another.

Emma, grandmother of six, wife of two years, offers these last words of advice to single grandmothers:

"There is no reason to sit home alone. The world is waiting for you out there if you just have the courage to go out and get involved with people. It just follows that companionship and love will find you."

CHAPTER 15

THE LAST WORD

Hand Out Hints

Remember when you were a girl stepping out the door and your mother offered tidbits of advice. She filled your ears with advice like "Don't forget to take a nickel for a phone call if he gets fresh," or "Now, you do have on clean underwear in case you get into an accident," or "Get home before eleven o'clock or your father will have a fit."

Well, this chapter is dedicated to words of advice, but these words are not from your mother. These tips have been gleaned from grandmothers who have been in the mid-life mating scene and want you to profit from what they've learned.

From Glenda, who played the singles club scene for four years before meeting and marrying Harry: "If you respect yourself, he'll respect you. In most singles clubs, men outnumber women two to one, and there are always a few men who play the field. Don't fall into the habit of vying for their attention. Men lose respect for women who are too easy.

"I know this sounds like your mother talking, but I've seen some sensible women go ga-ga over guys. The guys use them, then laugh at them. Being friendly but aloof is more intriguing to most men. You are a valuable person. Take good care of yourself."

Elise adds to this: "Don't fall into the desperate category by advertising your availability. I have a friend, Dorothy, who decided she was ready to date after the death of her husband. She went on the market with high profile advertising.

"She dyed her dark hair blond, piled on eyeliner and blusher until she looked like an overage hooker. She'd worn tasteful clothes before, but suddenly she began wearing fashions that would have better befitted her daughters. Skirts too short, sweaters too tight, heels too high, and earrings that brushed her shoulders. Dorothy is a disaster, but I just don't have the heart to tell her. She thinks she's a man killer."

Amanda's desperation didn't take the form of man-hunting with a vengeance. She found a man right off. She fell in love and hung on for dear life. Let's hear her story:

"I was 56 years old. I was lonely and hungry for affection when I met Con, a charming and vital pubic relations man. He came on like a freight train; and I was so smitten I would have turned myself inside out for this man.

"It sounds very dumb to be saying that, at 56, I was

trying to base a relationship on physical affection. I did like his brain, but I'd had so little affection for the past twenty years of a loveless marriage, I was ready for love.

"I was so anxious to keep this guy coming around that I completely submerged my own personality. I was loving. I was giving. I was caring. Hell, I was anything he wanted, a chameleon. I didn't need his money; I make good money on my own. I was simply in love with the kind of love you find in bodice-ripping novels.

"Nothing was too good for Con. I was sympathetic to his faults and never once did I lose my temper. And rarely did I express an opinion that was contrary to his. I thought we were perfectly matched and attuned to each other.

"When he wrote me a letter saying it was over; that the magic and excitement had gone out of our relationship, I thought of suicide. I felt like the fool of fools and that I had no future.

"Looking back on it, I can't believe I actually thought of suicide. I was the woman with everything to live for.

"It took a male friend to talk to me, look straight in my eyes and say, 'You're worth ten of him. He's a jerk, so don't make a saint out of him. He's nothing and you're everything. It's over, and you're well rid of him. Go on from this point and keep going. You're going to be just fine if you give yourself a chance.'

"My male friend stood by me and escorted me to social events. He acted the part of the devoted swain so well that he convinced the entire city.

"Eventually I met someone so wonderful, someone

with whom I could be myself and could share my life
with. I will never play act again. My longtime friend
was in the wings cheering me on. I am so perfectly
happy now I can't imagine why I let that man make me
so unhappy."

Occasionally we get locked into patterns of choice.
Don't be afraid to change, several mid-life ladies advise.

Nan, an attractive widow in her late fifties, says,
"Look beyond the covering of a man. Make an effort to
find what is underneath. Be willing to expand your
horizons. I watched a friend meet and marry a man who
was a look-alike to her dead husband. She made the
mistake of believing that if the outside was similar, the
inside was, too. It was not, and the marriage is a disaster."

Sharon follows along this same line. "When I was a
girl, I married a gorgeous guy with black curly hair and
blue eyes. I was instantly attracted to him because he
reminded me of my first love, who had black curly hair
and deep blue eyes. The marriage was a mistake from
day one.

"I am divorced now and am attracted to a fellow in
our church group. He has dark hair and deep blue eyes.
I'm not going to make the same mistake again. Going
for a physical type without really getting to know the
man himself is girl stuff, and I'm finally a grown woman
now."

Toni wasn't attracted to the outside of a man, but
she found herself being drawn to the same personality
type.

"I went through a terrible marriage and an equally
terrible divorce," she said. "After several years of coun-

seling, I felt able to get back into the dating world. Through work I met Norm, a deep-thinking, articulate supervisor in the next department. My heart began pitter-pattering every time he came near. When he asked me for a date, I accepted. We dated for several months.

"One evening after he'd dropped me off, I sat down to think about what might become a relationship. I listed Norm's good qualities and his bad qualities. When I looked over the list, I realized that Norm's qualities were very similar to those of my former husband. I remember a counselor cautioning me not to let a pattern of choice develop, and that was exactly what I was doing. I was getting right back into a relationship that would be emotionally devastating. I continued to date Norm for some time, but eventually we stopped seeing each other. I wasn't about to make the same mistake twice."

Some women share the traditional views: From Wynette, a grandmother in her fifties: "Be a good listener. Women have to be, however if you're a good listener, and he's not, get rid of the guy. A man who won't listen to you is not interested in you as a person. What he's interested in is himself, and this kind of man is not a good companion."

The advice given by Frances is pointed: "Remember that the Other Woman isn't always a young blonde goddess. It could be you. Don't let yourself get involved with a married man. Maybe the chemistry is a high buzz, but remember what every woman knows deep in her heart: 'If he cheats on his wife, he'll cheat on you.' That sounds hokey, and sure, I know that most of the

best men are married men, but don't fall into the trap. It
will only end in pain."

Others offer cautions about traditions:

Anna: "Older fellows who are widowed or divorced have gotten used to a woman taking care of
them. Often, when a mate dies, the man replaces her
immediately, and it's not for love. It's for maid service.
It's okay to like taking care of a guy, but make sure that
you get your share of the loving care."

Dixie: "Amen to those words. I am really fond of
Harve, and I like to cook for him, but he's begun to expect
supper to be on the table at 6 P.M. He shows up at my
house, ready to eat. I find myself rushing home from
work to prepare dinner. After dinner, while I clean up the
kitchen, he sits and watches sports on my TV. By the time
I've gotten through, he's fallen asleep. Eventually, he
wakes up and kisses me goodbye and goes home.

"I've finally awakened to the fact that he has all the
perks of marriage without responsibility. I love this guy,
but I'm definitely getting hostile. Next week, I plan
several outings with women friends. He's going to be
hungry, but maybe it will shake some sense into him."

Charmaine: "The night he left some laundry for me
to do was the night I came to my senses. I just wasn't
available the next time he appeared on my doorstep.
Luckily, I wasn't into the relationship so far that it hurt
to break it off. He wanted me to take right over where his
wife left off. Baloney to that. A new relationship needs
new habits, I say."

Most mature women are more concerned with self-
growth than are the men of their age group. Here are
some comments from women who think that self-
growth should never stop.

Teddi: "If you are dating a guy who never wants to explore new options or new activities, then you'll find yourself in a stagnant situation. Remove yourself before you begin to grow old with him."

Norma: "Howie and I are in our sixties. He believes that we are too old to travel outside this country. I say we're not. I'm planning a trip for two to Europe next year. He's dragging his feet, but he says he will go. I really love him for that. At least he's trying. If he's totally miserable, I won't push, but I want him to have the opportunity to see beyond his community. Going with a guy who won't even consider new things can really drag a woman down, unless, of course, she's in a similar rut. I'll never stop being curious about the world around me, and I simply can't stand a man who stubbornly refuses to expand his knowledge."

Maye: "Develop a new skill. If you don't play bridge, take it up. If you've always felt you have two left feet, sign up for some ballroom dancing instructions or square dancing sessions. Folk dancing is fascinating, and you don't need a partner. If you've cooked meat and potatoes all your married life, try some gourmet cooking classes. Women who do something well, even if it's baking dynamite brownies, give off a high level of energy, and men are attracted to this.

"If you've never entertained, here's your chance to learn a new skill that will pay off. Begin by giving a small dinner party or maybe a Christmas party for your apartment house or condo cluster. Keep it simple and keep it fun. Entertaining is a great way to get new people into your life."

Life is a series of compromises, some good, some not so good. Here are some words of wisdom from women who have faced challenges in coming to terms with less than a perfect relationship.

Betty: "When Henry and I were going together, he told me that he was impotent because of a physical problem. I am 64 years old. My late husband and I had a good sexual relationship up until the time he died three years ago.

"Henry and I are good buddies. We go places in his motor home, have a lot of fun with people we meet in Arizona during the winter and have our friends here to go dancing and dining with. I told him that, at my age, companionship and affection, were what I wanted most in a relationship. I know many women wouldn't settle for a non-physical relationship, but I am happy with Henry. We sleep together in the same bed; he cuddles with me and although there is no sex, our relationship is warm, pleasant and affectionate. I've compromised, but I do not feel I have lost out."

Judy: "Dale's not anyone my mother would have approved of, but I'm the mother now, and I can do anything I want to do. Dale can be boistrous to the point of crude. His intellect doesn't match mine, but he's smart in ways I never was. We have a good time together, and we have developed our own circle of friends. It isn't ideal, but I'm happy within the relationship we've formed. So what if my friends raise their eyebrows? I like Dale. He's good to me, and he's good to my kids. My grandchildren adore him."

Theresa: "I know women who marry much younger men get laughed at. That's unfortunate. Jeff and I love each other. He respects me for my age and quality of life; I respect him for his vitality and youth. We fit."

From the most contented recently married mid-life

woman I know—myself: Before you enter the mid-life dating world, learn how to be happy within yourself because only you are ultimately responsible for your own happiness. If you're content and satisfied within yourself, your aura and energy will attract the most wonderful people because happiness is infectious.